GOD AND FAITH

God and Faith

*Thinking About God with Keith Ward:
A Research Seminar Textbook*

EDITED BY IAN S. MARKHAM
AND J. D. BAUMAN

☙PICKWICK *Publications* · Eugene, Oregon

GOD AND FAITH
Thinking About God with Keith Ward: A Research Seminar Textbook

Copyright © 2025 Wipf and Stock Publishers. All rights reserved. Except for brief quotations in critical publications or reviews, no part of this book may be reproduced in any manner without prior written permission from the publisher. Write: Permissions, Wipf and Stock Publishers, 199 W. 8th Ave., Suite 3, Eugene, OR 97401.

Pickwick Publications
An Imprint of Wipf and Stock Publishers
199 W. 8th Ave., Suite 3
Eugene, OR 97401

www.wipfandstock.com

PAPERBACK ISBN: 979-8-3852-2029-8
HARDCOVER ISBN: 979-8-3852-2030-4
EBOOK ISBN: 979-8-3852-2031-1

Cataloguing-in-Publication data:

Names: Markham, Ian S. [editor．] | Bauman, J. D. [editor].

Title: God and faith : thinking about God with Keith Ward: a research seminar textbook / Ian S. Markham and J. D. Bauman.

Description: Eugene, OR: Pickwick Publications, 2025 | Includes bibliographical references and index.

Identifiers: ISBN 979-8-3852-2029-8 (paperback) | ISBN 979-8-3852-2030-4 (hardcover) | ISBN 979-8-3852-2031-1 (ebook)

Subjects: LCSH: Ward, Keith, 1938–. | Theology. | Philosophical theology. | Religion—Philosophy. | Philosophy and religion.

Classification: BR127 M37 2025 (paperback) | BR127 (ebook)

03/28/25

Unless otherwise stated, all scripture quotations are taken from the New Revised Standard Version Updated Edition. Copyright © 2021 National Council of Churches of Christ in the United States of America. Used by permission. All rights reserved worldwide.

Contents

List of Contributors | vii

Preface | ix

1   The Methodology of Keith Ward | 1
          IAN S. MARKHAM

     Keith Ward's Response to Ian S. Markham | 21
     Discussion Questions | 23

2   Probing Ward's Personal Idealism: Faith, Foundation, or Regulative Ideal? | 24
          PHILIP CLAYTON AND JAEHA WOO

     Keith Ward's Response to Philip Clayton and Jaeha Woo | 41
     Discussion Questions | 43

3   Hope Springs Eternal: Grounding a Theology of Divine Hope in the Work of Keith Ward | 44
          WM. CURTIS HOLTZEN

     Keith Ward's Response to Wm. Curtis Holtzen | 63
     Discussion Questions | 65

4   Keith Ward and a Metaphysics of Love | 66
          THOMAS JAY OORD

     Keith Ward's Response to Thomas Jay Oord | 85
     Discussion Questions | 87

5   Keith Ward and Pedagogy | 88
        J'ANNINE JOBLING

     Keith Ward's Response to J'annine Jobling | 107

     Discussion Questions | 109

6   Possibility, Value, and Mind: The Entangled Heart of Keith Ward's Philosophical Theology | 110
        ANDREW M. DAVIS

     Keith Ward's Response to Andrew M. Davis | 126

     Discussion Questions | 128

7   Keith Ward on Comparative Theology and Religious Pluralism: A Catholic Appreciation | 129
        PETER C. PHAN

     Keith Ward's Response to Peter C. Phan | 148

     Discussion Questions | 150

Glossary | 151

Index | 157

List of Contributors

Keith Ward is the emeritus regius professor of divinity at the University of Oxford; he is the author of numerous books. He has an international profile for his work on idealism, comparative theology, and science and religion.

Philip Clayton holds the Ingraham chair at Claremont School of Theology. He specializes in the philosophy of science, comparative theology, and has written numerous books.

Jaeha Woo is a researcher in religion and philosophy. He holds a PhD from the Claremont School of Theology.

Wm. Curtis Holtzen is professor of philosophy and theology at Hope International University. Best known for this book *The God Who Trusts: A Relational Theology of Divine Faith, Hope and Love*, he has a deep interest in the relationship between science and religion.

Thomas Jay Oord directs the doctoral program at Northwind Theological Seminary and the Center for Open and Relational Theology. He has an international reputation for his advocacy for open theism. He is the author of numerous books.

J'annine Jobling is a senior lecturer at the University of Liverpool in the UK. She has written on spirituality, fantasy, feminist theology, and biblical hermeneutics. Her more recent work has focused on educational skills.

Andrew M. Davis is academic and research director at the Center for Process Studies. He is a specialist in process philosophy and theology.

Peter C. Phan is a professor at Georgetown University, where he holds the Ignacio Ellacuría chair of Catholic social thought. He specializes in theology, eschatology, comparative theology, and interreligious dialogue.

LIST OF CONTRIBUTORS

THE EDITORS

Ian S. Markham is the dean and president of Virginia Theological Seminary and professor of theology and ethics. He has written extensively on theological methodology, Christian ethics, and Christian doctrine.

J. D. Bauman is a student at Virginia Theological Seminary with a training in philosophy of religion and theology. He is the director of Effective Altruism for Christians.

Preface

WHEN I WAS FIFTEEN YEARS OLD, *Why There Almost Certainly Is a God* opened a gateway to the vast and fascinating world of philosophy of religion. It ignited in me a deep curiosity about philosophical issues within religion, science, and theology. Now, as a graduate student in theology, Keith Ward's writings continue to challenge me as well as my professors and peers. With over fifty books to his name, the emeritus regius professor of divinity at the University of Oxford is among the most creative and influential theologians of our time.

This book is designed to capture the essence of Ward's thought and invite readers into a dynamic conversation about some of the toughest theological questions. Unlike traditional books that focus on a single sustained argument, this book presents a range of perspectives, encouraging critical reflection and engagement with diverse voices.

Each chapter features an essay from a distinguished scholar who engages with a specific aspect of Keith Ward's thought. These essays are followed by a response from Ward himself, creating a dialogue that is uniquely insightful and thought-provoking. At the end of each chapter, you will find critical reflection questions designed to provoke thought and discussion by graduate-level students and readers.

In the opening chapter, Ian S. Markham explores Keith Ward's unique methodological approach. Markham discusses how Ward employs a synthesis of rational inquiry and faith-based reasoning, navigating between adherence to doctrinal orthodoxy and openness to new insights from various fields of study, including science and other religious traditions.

Philip Clayton and Jaeha Woo delve into Ward's concept of personal idealism, examining whether it serves as a foundational belief for faith or as an interpretive hypothesis. They critically analyze Ward's claim that reality is fundamentally constituted by conscious experience (Mind) and goodness (Value), and explore the implications of this view for understanding faith and metaphysics.

Wm. Curtis Holtzen's essay argues that divine hope is a necessary and plausible attribute of God. He examines how Ward's conception of God—temporal, creatively cooperative, and affected by human freedom—supports the idea that God can have hope, particularly in working towards a loving relationship with free creatures.

Thomas Jay Oord makes the case that a religion focused on the theme of love can build on the foundation of Keith Ward's account of Idealism. He makes various proposals for Ward to consider, such as a strong mind-matter monism, which Ward declines to affirm.

J'annine Jobling argues how Ward's work is relevant to contemporary educational models. She explores how Ward's metaphysical account of Christianity—emphasizing faith, reason, diversity, and creativity—can inspire educational practices that resist marketization and instrumentalism, fostering environments of critical reflection, agency, and relational learning.

Andrew M. Davis delves into Keith Ward's philosophical idealism, focusing on the interrelation of possibility, value, and mind in his metaphysical framework. Davis highlights how Ward's view positions a cosmic Mind as the ultimate reality that encompasses all possibilities and values, asserting that this Mind, defined by goodness and love, necessarily creates and guides the universe.

Peter C. Phan offers a Catholic perspective on Ward's approach to comparative theology and religious pluralism. He examines how Ward's theology promotes mutual understanding and cooperation among different faiths while maintaining a commitment to Christian revelation.

Each chapter concludes with a set of critical reflection questions designed to encourage deeper reflection or discussion. To aid readers in navigating the complex ideas and terminology discussed in the book, terms are provided at the back for easy reference to specific topics and themes.

This book presents a unique opportunity for readers and students to engage with world-class scholars in a Socratic style. It is an essential resource for those wishing to deepen their understanding and participate in critical conversations on some of the most difficult questions in theology, religion, and science.

J. D. Bauman
Virginia Theological Seminary

1

The Methodology of Keith Ward[1]

IAN S. MARKHAM

Although tiresome, methodology remains a central arena for debate among theologians. It is tiresome because conclusions (what exactly is God like?) are much more interesting than endlessly discussing how we might start knowing what God is like. Yet the methodological divide in the academy is acute: today significant numbers of theologians insist that knowledge is ideological and the goal must be a theology that supports a justice-oriented outcome. Ward, while sympathetic to many of the political positions (so, for example, he supported the ordination of women and the inclusion of LGBT+ clergy), has a methodology grounded in a traditional "critical realist" aspiration, where we arrive an account of God that is in some sense closer to the truth than other metaphysical worldviews.

This paper explores the approach of Keith Ward and places his approach in conversation with the alternatives. We start by posing the challenge of many contemporary approaches before moving to offer an account of his method. The paper concludes by defending the Wardian approach.

KNOWING AND IDEOLOGY

Perhaps we now have a majority of theologians, certainly in America, who are showing a sensitivity to the complex relationship between knowing and

---

1. This is my second attempt to visit the methodology of Keith Ward. The first is found in Markham, *Theology of Engagement*. I have in places drawn on some of my earlier arguments.

ideology. This is the position that asserts *knowledge claims often reflect vested interests*. The roots of this approach, in the modern period, are in Karl Marx. He was the one who insisted that the economic base was responsible for the superstructure that included law, philosophy, and religion. In a capitalist economy, Marx argued, the unjust economic relationships generate the religious ideas that support those unjust relations. A classic illustration is the focus on a "pietist" gospel (by which I mean, the focus is individual salvation beyond the grave and the primary sins are sexual) which came to the fore in the nineteenth century in Britain and birthed the verse of "all things bright and beautiful" (which fortunately is no longer sung).

> *The rich man in his castle, the poor man at his gate*
> *God made them, high and lowly, and ordered their estate.*[2]

The combination of God ordering the status of humanity, coupled with sin having no social dimension, and salvation being entirely other worldly does look like a theology that serves the interests of the rich in a capitalist society.

Once this idea gained traction, others started asking the question: Whose interests are served by this theology? Feminist theology developed an entire trajectory that saw in the traditional dualisms—between body and spirit, and God and the world—a theology that supported patriarchy. Queer theologians argued that the consistent denigration of the body had implications for LGBT+ persons. Postcolonial theologians see empire as a conditioning theme of much Anglican theology. More recently, Willie James Jennings has argued that certain Christian themes, such as creation and providence, were framed as historical justifications for white power over black flesh.[3]

Persuaded of this danger, some revisionist theologians have turned the entire task of theology around. Gordon Kaufman is a good illustration. Kaufman explains that there are four "fundamental dimensions" of his faith and piety that are assumed in his theological system. He writes:

> These are (a) my deep sense of the ultimate mystery of life; (b) my feelings of profound gratitude for the gift of humanness and the great diversity which it manifests; (c) my belief (with this diversity especially in mind) in the continuing importance of the central

---

2. The words are by Cecil Frances Alexander and were first published in her *Hymns for Little Children* in 1848.

3. See Jennings, *The Christian Imagination*.

Christian moral demand that we love and care for not only our neighbors but even our enemies; and (d) my conviction (closely connected with this last point) that the principal Christian symbols continue to provide a significant resource for the orientation of human life.[4]

Kaufman admits that much of his theology is "agnostic."[5] He wants to reinterpret the symbol "God" so that it is less oppressive (to the poor, the marginalized, women) and yet still places some demand on humanity. So, "God" becomes "a norm or criterion or reality—what I call an 'ultimate point of reference'—in terms of which all else may be assessed and understood."[6]

Now the task is not to seek the truth of what God might be like, but instead create a theology that has a commitment to justice at the core. Theology becomes a constructive task of creating ways of thinking that support just relationships in respect to race, the environment, and the poor. It is an ultimate point of reference that judges our values, hopes, and aspirations in this life. Kaufman is opposed to any dualism that sets God against this world, life against heaven, or nature against spirit.[7] Given that all human theology is a human construct, we need not be afraid of reinventing our concept of God so that it more obviously affirms life and justice. The "God" symbol, explains Kaufman, "must be understood as a product of human imagination."[8] This frees us up to seek an appropriate redefinition of it. Along with God, Christology too is revisited. Kaufman wants a wider Christology in which "Christ" brings "a new communal ethos in history."[9] And on ecclesiology, Kaufman sees the churches as a "community of reconciliation and humanization."[10]

Theology is no longer an attempt to formulate an account of God that is plausible and might make sense to the inquiring mind. But theology has become an attempt to create a language that will challenge prejudice and underpin justice.

---

4. Kaufman, *In Face of Mystery*, xii.
5. Kaufman, *In Face of Mystery*, xiii.
6. Kaufman, *In Face of Mystery*, 28.
7. Kaufman, *In Face of Mystery*, 326.
8. Kaufman, *In Face of Mystery*, 39.
9. Kaufman, *In Face of Mystery*, 396.
10. Kaufman, *In Face of Mystery*, 442.

It is against this backdrop that we turn to the work of Keith Ward. The question we must have is this: Is the Ward approach to theology outmoded and misguided? We will examine his approach under five headings—critical realism with a community sensitivity, engagement of all faith traditions, engagement with science, Christian doctrine, and speculative suggestions.

CRITICAL REALISM WITH A COMMUNITY SENSITIVITY

Ward wants to weave a commitment to critical realism (by which I mean some form of commitment to the possibility of a correspondence theory of truth, even though there are many influences that are acting on us) with a Wittgensteinian sympathy to the significance of communities shaping our worldview. To do this, he needs to walk a very fine (and difficult) line.

It was in one of his earliest works, *Concept of God*, he is clearly assuming a Wittgensteinian framework. In *Religion and Revelation*, he returns to Wittgenstein and asserts that there are certain "frameworks" that are not justified rationally but simply assumed. Ward writes:

> Worship and prayer, for example, are natural practices by which humans relate to the world of their experience in specific ways. They do not, as such, stand in need of justification, for they are rooted in basic attitudes of awe, reverence, gratitude and dependence, which show themselves in human behavior. They form the basis for developing sets of concepts which aim to provide illuminating descriptions of how the world is and of how humans ought to live. At that stage they become subject to rational inquiry and assessment.[11]

So, stage one, we have a set of practices within a certain community; and then, stage two, these practices create descriptions—"truth claims"—that then become subject to the rigors of rationality.

One challenge for Ward is that while conceding that there are different practices in different communities (which do not need justification), he also wants to be able to compare and analyze the theologies of these different communities. And when he writes about theological analysis, he takes two very clear stands. The first is that there are some universal rational criteria; and the second is that the traditional processes of seeking a coherent worldview with explanatory power work. On the first, he writes firmly:

---

11. Ward, *Religion and Revelation*, 11

> if one asks to what "tradition" these basic criteria of rationality—self-consistency, coherence with other knowledge, and adequacy to available data—belong, the answer must be that they belong to the tradition of being human, as such. . . . [T]hey are principles of rationality which are built into the necessary structure of human social life, and thus function as desirable ideals for any community that wishes to survive for any length of time.[12]

Against Grace Jantzen, for example, Ward rejects the assumption that the affirmation of rationality is linked to gender or power.[13] Instead, all humans who seek to understand the world will affirm the principle, for example, that "self-contradictory truth claims cannot be true." He is aware that there is a history to logic (he was, after all, a professor of logic at the University of Glasgow); but presumably, this was simply humanity unpacking the structures that underpin effective communication. Although there are scholars who talk of a Buddhist logic, say, Ward would assert that *any* "logic" must build on certain fundamentals of rationality.

On the second, he starts his *Rational Theology and the Creativity of God* in the following way:

> These two tasks—of expounding the idea of God and of establishing the rationality and moral importance of belief in God—go together. Without a clear idea of God, one cannot be sure of what, exactly, one is looking for reasons to accept. And without a clear account of the reasons for belief, one cannot be sure of what it is that one has established as the conclusions of those reasoning.[14]

This seems clear enough. One needs to explain what one means by the word "God"—so some coherent account is needed; and then one can provide reasons for the existence of God (why believing in such an entity explains the complexity of the world). In *Religion and Revelation*, he expands on this approach, when he writes:

> There are some very basic rational criteria which can be brought to bear upon all claims to truth, in religion as elsewhere. Rationality involves the use of intelligent capacities, including the capacity to register information correctly, to compare similar pieces of information, to deduce and infer in accordance with rules of logic and relate means to ends effectively. A rational person can act on a

---

12. Ward, *Religion and Revelation*, 320
13. See Jantzen, *Becoming Divine*.
14. Ward, *Rational Theology and the Creativity of God*, 1.

consciously formulated principle in order to attain an intended goal.... Such simple forms of reasoning are necessary to any form of intelligently ordered social life. They are not, and cannot be, culturally relative.[15]

In his four-volume comparative theology he applies these principles of rationality to each religious thinker with whom he engages. And it feels as if his commitment to rationality seems to trump his commitment to honoring the practices of traditions as not in need of justification. So, for example, in his discussion of Mohammed Iqbal's account of God, he identifies three such accounts—the immanent Infinite, the universe as the character of the cosmic Self, and the creative co-worker with finite selves. He worries that this might be incoherent; and then he defends Iqbal by suggesting, rather nervously, that there are resonances with the Trinity.[16] It is not necessary to determine whether Ward's critique of Iqbal is right or not (although, let me parenthetically note, I think Ward is right), the point is that it seems that reason is primary, and the community worldview is secondary.

Perhaps the best way of seeing these two elements is to say that Ward wants to make experience primary and theology as a second-order engagement with religious experience. So, the various experiences of God that express themselves in religious practice underpin all attempts to talk about God. This is really a fairly long way from Wittgenstein. The element of Wittgenstein Ward wants to affirm is that communities form languages that attempt to describe their experiences. But he wants to completely reject any cultural relativism or lazy postmodernism; and he sees no problem in reflecting on the potential incoherence of other religious traditions.

ENGAGEMENT OF OTHER RELIGIOUS TRADITIONS

Ward affirms the classic assumption that all truth belongs to God. Therefore, wherever truth is found, then that truth is part of the truth of God. At the start of his *Religion and Revelation*, he writes: "The most distinctive feature of the book is that it espouses a comparative method, examining the idea of revelation as it is found both in the primal religious traditions and in the great canonical traditions of the world."[17] He feels it is impor-

---

15. Ward, *Religion and Revelation*, 319.
16. Ward, *Religion and Creation*, 66–68.
17. Ward, *Religion and Revelation*, 1.

tant to engage with religious diversity because God is the God of the whole world. He suspects there are insights found in other religious traditions that Christians can learn from.

He is an advocate of an "open theology." He explains:

> One might perhaps speak of an "open theology," which can be characterized by six main features. It will seek a convergence of common core beliefs, clarifying the deep arguments which underlie diverse cultural traditions. It will seek to learn from complementary beliefs in other traditions, expecting that there are forms of revelation one's own tradition does not express. It will be prepared to reinterpret its belief in the light of new, well-established factual and moral beliefs. It will accept the full right of diverse belief-systems to exist, as long as they do not cause avoidable injury or harm to innocent sentient beings. It will encourage a dialogue with conflicting and dissenting views, being prepared to confront its own tradition with critical questions arising out of such views. And it will try to develop a sensitivity to the historical and cultural contexts of the formulation of its own beliefs, with a preparedness to continue developing new insights in new cultural situations.[18]

This is a good summary of Ward's work in the area of interreligious engagement. The "convergence of common core beliefs" is seen in his *Images of Eternity*, where he identifies the key elements shared across different religious traditions. "Learning from complementary beliefs in other traditions" is interesting. So, for Ward, there are insights in other faith traditions that are compatible with orthodox Christianity but not explicitly found in Christianity. Perhaps the Buddhist doctrine of "non-attachment" (given the ephemeral nature of everything it is important that we avoid certain attachments—things, doctrines, rituals, and the self) is an insight that is compatible with the doctrine of the incarnation. The willingness to "reinterpret" our tradition in the light of "new, well-established factual and moral beliefs" is seen in the affirmation of the theory of evolution rather than a version of creationism or in the inclusion of LGBT+ persons. The next two owe much to the classic liberal tradition of John Stuart Mill. "The full right of diverse belief-systems to exist" and "encouraging dialogue" are part of the liberal affirmation of the principle of toleration because in disagreement we can learn from difference. The last "awareness of the cultural conditioning of our beliefs" is often alluded to in Ward's work. Although he does not identify with the anxiety that knowledge can be ideology, he

18. Ward, *Religion and Revelation*, 339–40.

does recognize that culture is a major influence. So, he would recognize that being white, male, and an Oxford professor does create a vantage point that must influence one's worldview. The nineteenth-century liberal values do not seem to work or to be appropriate when you are up against systemic racism or abject poverty.

His four-volume comparative theology was written right at the end of the last century. Interestingly, the series continues to stand alone. Part of the argument of this paper is that the project did not generate imitators partly because the academy chose to focus on the political and social dimensions of one's vantage point. Knowledge became local and political. Ward's comparative theology is global and metaphysical. For many theologians, the sixth principle became primary. Thus, understanding how a context of privilege generates a theology of privilege was the territory on which so many theologians chose to work. At the end of the paper, I shall return to these issues.

ENGAGING WITH SCIENCE

It is the same conviction about all truth being part of God's truth that made Keith Ward develop a significant corpus of writing on science. Indeed, his recent emphasis on "idealism" is best seen as a culmination of this trajectory. For Ward, idealism captures an important and key idea. Mind or spirit is primary. Consciousness is not reducible to brain states. God existed prior to the creation of matter. Therefore, some form of idealism is central.

Although he is very careful (whenever Ward writes about science, he wants to make sure that he doesn't overstate the implications of, say, physics for theology), he is sympathetic to the view that discoveries in quantum mechanics are compatible with, if not suggestive of, some form of idealism. Given this, we have a good foundation on which apologetics can build. The metaphysic that theism would affirm, namely, the primacy of the spiritual over the material, is compatible with one of the most exciting branches of contemporary science.

Quantum mechanics also creates possibilities for divine action. At the very least the reductionist deterministic universe is clearly not true. Ward believes that a more dynamic picture of the universe is made possible. He writes, "The theory of cosmic evolution encourages us to think of the story of the expanding universe as the development of new and richer forms of beauty and wisdom, strictly unpredictable from their antecedents, but always remaining within the basic parameters of fundamental physical constraints, general forms of patterned relationships which allow and even encourage the construction of more complex hierarchies of existence."[19] In his book *Divine Action*, Ward defends miracle and providence using the language of contemporary science. Drawing an analogy with human action, where mind exercises agency through the material body, so God exercises agency through the material world.

Methodologically, Ward is taking scientific insights and incorporating them into the theistic narrative. To the objection that one is linking one's account of Christianity to a particular scientific model, which is bound to change, he would, presumably, concede this possibility. One is always linking theism to the best scientific models of one's time; and one is resigned to the fact that in a hundred years time the limitations of those models will require a change in one's account of God. However, he prefers to take the risk to link his theology to a model rather than leave countless people with the impression that theology cannot make any connection with science. It is better to accept that the theological account will change as the science changes than to disregard the truth that is being learned through scientific inquiry.

At times when a scientific insight is fairly settled, then he believes that it would be irresponsible to refuse to accommodate that insight. Granted, there are continuing debates about the precise nature of evolution, however, it is a settled conclusion of all reputable sciences that some form of natural selection did occur over a long period of time in the generation of species on planet earth. Therefore, evolution must be accommodated. Interestingly, he is now arguing for a comparable shift in our perspective of the second coming of Jesus. In the same way that we have read the creation narratives in the light of the truth of evolution, so we need to read the apocalyptic narratives in the light of the truth of the scientific narrative for the future of the universe. Christians in the New Testament expected the return of Jesus in their lifetime. This expectation is clearly not true. Instead, we now know that in all likelihood humanity is unlikely to survive the death of our sun in approximately four billion years time (although with the increasing heat of the sun we will have significant problems in a billion years time). This, for Ward, is a fairly settled scientific insight. Therefore, argues Ward, we should interpret the language about the second coming to refer to the culmination of the project of creation in the ultimate death of our universe and to our

---

19. Ward, *God, Faith and the New Millennium*, 74.

own judgment at death; all the talk about Jesus returning on the clouds to take the elect with him to glory should be demythologized.[20]

Two factors are at work in Ward's methodology in this area. We have already met the first; this is the important insight that truth is always of God and should be accommodated by the theologian. The second is a new factor: this is apologetics. Ward believes that there is an opportunity here. Science coincides with spirituality.

CHRISTIAN DOCTRINE

With this passion for interreligious engagement and for integrating scientific insights, one might suspect that Ward is less interested in traditional doctrine. However, this is not the case at all. In many respects, he is surprisingly orthodox. There are passages in Ward that are surprising.

Take, for example, the Eucharist. Using a complex, almost Wittgenstenian account of the significance of the bread and wine in the Eucharist for the Christian community, he concludes that one can properly use the term "transubstantiation."[21] His argument takes the following form. First, the Eucharist is properly understood as symbolic. In an echo of Paul Tillich, he explains, "a symbol, in this sense, participates in and conveys the reality which it symbolizes."[22] Second, the Eucharist for the Christian community functions as a vehicle for participating in the redeeming work of God. He writes that when Jesus initiates the practice, he

> gives the disciples a foreshadowing symbol of that revealing and redeeming act. The broken bread presents both the sacrifice of the faithful servant and the divine passion. The wine originates a new covenant, sealed by the sacrifice of Jesus, already completed in intention, by which the life of the eternal Word begins to transform the lives of men and women. Every subsequent celebration of that supper makes present the same reality, whose significance is greatly enriched by knowledge of the resurrection and outpouring of the Spirit.[23]

---

20. This argument is made in the commencement address at Virginia Theological Seminary in May 2017.

21. For a fuller discussion of Ward's view of the sacraments, see Markham, *Understanding Christian Doctrine*.

22. Ward, *Religion and Community*, 194.

23. Ward, *Religion and Community*, 195–96.

The third step is to advocate for what it calls a relational model rather than a mechanical model. When you think of bread, Ward argues, it is not just a chemical compound, but instead it is a "product of sowing, growing, reaping, and baking, and so of a joining of natural forces with human cultivation."[24] The role of people and the purpose of the break are key properties of the bread. Therefore, in the fourth step:

> One might then say that, if bread is used in a ritual context, its essence (its substance in the sense of that which defines what it essentially is) is significantly changed. The mode of preparation remains the same, and yet part of that preparation becomes its setting apart by an act of blessing. By that act, it is consecrated to God set apart from common use. It is no longer ordinary bread, and its intended purpose becomes quite different.[25]

This is, for Ward, transubstantiation. He writes, "If one means that the essential nature of the bread has changed, even though all its essential properties remain the same."[26] The purpose of this bread is to enable the divine life to become part of the worshiper. Now the final fifth step is to explain how and in what sense is Christ present in the sacrament. Ward argues that the basic operation is the same as the incarnation. In the incarnation, the Eternal Word (the second person of the Trinity) becomes present in the human life of Jesus. In the Eucharist, the Eternal Word becomes present in the bread and wine. Ward writes:

> Even though the particular acts of the Word in Jesus are not exactly repeatable (there will never again be a young man teaching in a remote province of the Roman Empire) there is a sense in which the liberating action of the Word in Jesus can be repeated in different contexts. What is present on the altar is the eternal Christ in the particular form he took in Jesus, acting to convey divine love and power as he did in Jesus.[27]

In these five steps, we have Ward's account of the Eucharist. From the divine perspective, God, through the Spirit, is making the Eternal Word present in a distinctive way in the bread and wine. From the human perspective, the liturgical context and the prayer of consecration imbues the bread with

---

24. Ward, *Religion and Community*, 197.
25. Ward, *Religion and Community*, 197.
26. Ward, *Religion and Community*, 198.
27. Ward, *Religion and Community*, 199.

a new and distinctive purpose. In so doing, we can properly speak of the bread changing into the body and blood of Jesus.

Methodologically, one sees Ward grapple with a doctrine and work as hard as he can to formulate an account that is philosophically sophisticated and simultaneously "orthodox." It isn't an Ulrich Zwingli account of a memorial. He actually uses the Roman Catholic language of "transubstantiation." He wants to firmly identify with a traditional form of Christianity, even if the defense of the Eucharist is in many ways very modern.

Another Ward surprise is the virgin birth. Ward is inclined to accept the veracity of the tradition that this occurred. It is worth quoting his reasoning at length. He writes:

> If Jesus was born while Mary was a virgin, that would certainly be a miracle. While it is just possible for women to give birth to females by parthenogenesis (without insemination by a male), women just do not have the Y chromosome that is necessary to produce a male child. If this happened, it is not possible within the limits of the laws of nature, so those laws must have been suspended. I have already suggested that, so far as science goes, God could suspend natural laws occasionally, for a good enough reason. Since the whole life of Jesus must be a miracle, in its exemption from sin, that seems a good enough reason for the birth of Jesus to be a miracle. This, after all, is claimed to be the decisive act of God on this planet to restore the divine purpose of creation and liberate humanity from its bondage to sin. So it is not just a rare event, but a totally unique one. I am therefore inclined to accept that Jesus was, as the Apostles' Creed puts it, "born of the Virgin Mary."[28]

Now what is interesting about this justification for the doctrine of the virgin birth is what is absent. This passage is preceded by an analysis of the Gospel narratives. Then he considers the science, moves towards the possibility of a distinctive divine action, offers a rationale in terms of the significance of the life of Jesus, and concludes therefore it is likely. Do note, there is no appeal to authority or to the traditions of the church. Science and reason come to the fore.

From the virgin birth, we naturally come to Christology. It seems strange in many ways that Ward works with such zeal to defend many traditional positions yet has actually taken a variety of positions on Christ. It is clear that his understanding of Christ has been modified in three of his books: *Divine Action, A Vision to Pursue,* and *Religion and Revelation.*

28. Ward, *God, Faith and the New Millennium*, 175.

The Methodology of Keith Ward

Ward explains the movement from *Divine Action* to *A Vision to Pursue* in the following way. Since he became a Christian, his instinct was to see Jesus as a human being "who obeyed God fully, knew and loved him intimately, and as a result was able to bring God close to others or even act in the place of God in regard to other people. He was a man wholly transparent to God, perhaps, and thus a perfected vehicle of divine love."[29] However, he explained, he wanted to explore the classical doctrine of the incarnation: he could see certain advantages, and therefore set out to defend an ontological doctrine of the incarnation in *Divine Action*. Methodologically, this is interesting. *Divine Action* is an experiment. He is exploring a "conceptual possibility" (in other words, the attempt to formulate a good case for a logically possible position). *Divine Action* defends a kenotic version of the incarnation. However, even in *Divine Action*, he is concerned about the ignorance Jesus shows when it comes to the unfolding of the "last days." In *A Vision to Pursue*, we have a much lower Christology—the perfect human who shows us God. However, in *Religion and Revelation*, he shifts again. In a footnote, he explains that any reader of *A Vision to Pursue* "will note a much more pronounced incarnational emphasis in this present work. I have become convinced that such an emphasis is necessary and possible, given a relatively small amendment of the previous analysis."[30] The account in *Religion and Revelation* continues to reject a Jesus who was omniscient, omnipotent, and consciously preexistent. Instead, he argues for an enhypostatic view of incarnation. Ward explains thus:

> What the life-perfectly-united-to-God shows is the nature and purpose of God. Jesus has a free mind and will, which makes its own decisions and performs its own creative actions. He is united to God in such a way that in freely obeying his distinctive calling, he expresses what God is, becoming a living revelation of Supreme value.[31]

Methodologically, we note the following. Ward wants to take the tradition seriously. He wants to be a priest who is faithful to the church. Yet his commitment to coherence and plausibility mean that he struggles with certain doctrines, supremely, with his understanding of Christ.

---

29. Ward, *A Vision to Pursue*, 49.
30. Ward, *Religion and Revelation*, 240.
31. Ward, *Religion and Revelation*, 272.

SPECULATIVE SUGGESTIONS

To conclude this summary of Ward, there are three areas that I want to highlight that reflect further on Ward's methodology. These three areas are a departure from the tradition. The first is life on other planets; the second is animal immortality; and the third is artificial intelligence.

The issue of life on other planets is one that has emerged in several places in Ward's writings. In *A Vision to Pursue*, Ward criticizes the work of Brian Hebblethwaite for his assertion that the uniqueness of the incarnation makes life on other planets impossible. Ward writes:

> The *reductio ad absurdum* of Hebblethwaite's view comes when he writes that "it is an implication of the Christian doctrine of the Incarnation, properly understood, that there are no other intelligent, personal creatures in God's creation than human beings here on earth." This is bad news for the multi-billion dollar United States programme for seeking out extra-terrestrial life forms. They could hire a Cambridge theologian to tell him that such forms are theologically impossible; and he would be much cheaper. Surely the time for such purely *a priori* assertions about empirical matters of fact ran out with Hegel's infamous proof that there could be no more planets in the solar system, just before another one was discovered.[32]

Ironically, the theological skepticism of Brian Hebblethwaite found a twenty-first-century ally in Simon Conway-Morris. Keith Ward summarizes Conway Morris arguing by explaining "that in our universe, given the basic laws and constraints upon which it has developed, carbon-based humanoids are the only sorts of intelligent beings that can exist. He further argues that the conditions for the existence of such life are so extremely rare that we are probably the only intelligent beings that exist even in a universe as large and old as this one."[33] Now, methodologically, Ward takes the scientific hesitation seriously. However, he is committed to the view that other forms of intelligent life do exist in this universe. Ward writes, "I am inclined to say that God did create other kinds of intelligent life and that it would be very odd if in all the galaxies in this universe there are no other kinds of intelligent life."[34] And his reasoning is interesting:

32. Ward, *A Vision to Pursue*, 83.

33. The summary of Conway Morris is taken from Ward, *Christ and the Cosmos*, 250. For Conway Morris, see Morris, *Life's Solution*.

34 Ward, *Christ and the Cosmos*, 250.

> My understanding of the unlimited love and power of God is such that I would think it quite possible for God to create many kinds of intelligent beings, and quite probably that God has done so. . . . What I am confident about, however, is that, logically speaking, there seems to be nothing incoherent in supposing that many sorts of intelligent beings could exist (Christians have, after all, often believed that there are angels and other "heavenly powers"). And if God's creation of this universe is free, then God might have created other universes. This makes the creation of this universe contingent, something God did not have to do. . . . It may seem a radical and to some an incredible and unnecessary claim that extraterrestrial intelligences exist. But it is not at all incredible, and it has in fact been part of the most traditional Christian beliefs to say that God did not have to create this universe, that humans did not have to sin, and that God could have redeemed humans without becoming incarnate. Thomas Aquinas certainly asserted all these propositions. So my argument does not depend upon positing extra-terrestrial beings, though our very recent discovery of the vast extent of the universe does help the imagination think that God may really be known by other beings in very different ways than those in which God is known by us.[35]

The background here is Ward's concern that using human images for the Trinity could be problematic and would be problematic if (or when) other intelligent life is found in the universe. The speculation here does have a theological point; in addition, the speculation is assuming a "traditional theological frame" concerning divine freedom to do otherwise (and Aquinas is invoked); and finally, he thinks it is more likely than not that life on other planets does exist.

Most of the tradition does not support animal immortality. However, Ward makes animal immortality essential to his theodicy. Indeed, he takes the view that theism cannot be true if there is no life beyond the grave. Again his reasoning is insightful:

> If there is no possibility of final transfiguration, any such talk can be no more than a self-deluding sham. If it is necessary that each sentient being must have the possibility of achieving an overwhelming good, then it is clear that there must be some form of life after earthly death. Despite the many pointers to the existence of God, theism would be falsified if physical death was the end, for then there could be no justification for the existence of this world.

---

35. Ward, *Christ and the Cosmos*, 250–51.

> However, if one supposes that every sentient being has an endless existence, which offers the prospect of supreme happiness, it is surely true that the sorrows and troubles of this life will seem very small by comparison. Immortality, for animals as well as humans, is a necessary condition of any acceptable theodicy; that necessity, together with all the other arguments for God, is one of the main reasons for being in immortality.[36]

For Ward, the supreme happiness of God's creatures is a key part of any adequate theodicy. Indeed, without the life to come, theodicy, for Ward, is impossible. Now given the close connection between animals and humanity, given the extent of the suffering in the non-human realm, he insists that both humans and animals must enjoy immortality.

Many questions are left unanswered. Animal immortality for our pet animals makes sense; but does it extend to the tick and the mosquito? And why stop at animals. Why not trees and streams? Trees suffer at the brutal acts of humanity; and trees have mechanisms of communication. But, methodologically, the achievement here is to place on the table an idea that extends the principle that suffering is redeemed in the life to come. And to his credit, this cannot just stop at human life. It extends further to the non-human realm.

The third illustration is consciousness and artificial intelligence. In his *Battle for the Soul*, Ward argues for an account of the soul—which is the location of purpose, agency, and moral decision-making—that is, in our current human state, linked to the material brain.[37] Ward claims that this view of the soul is implicit in the work of the thirteenth-century Dominican Friar Thomas Aquinas. He writes:

> If the human soul is, as Aquinas taught, the basic principle of a rational organism, the power of thought and understanding, then it can easily be seen as developing continuously from lower, non-rational or non-cognitive, forms of life. In modern terminology, we might say that, when the brain reaches a certain level of complexity, the power of conceptual thought, of reasoning and thinking, begins to exist; and that is when a rational soul begins to be. The rational soul is that which has the power of understanding.[38]

---

36. Ward, *Rational Theology and the Creativity of God*, 201–2.

37. I defend Ward's account of personhood and the possibility of consciousness and AI in Markham, "The Plugged-in Church."

38. Ward, *The Battle for the Soul*, 52.

So, Ward has the following picture. As our brain develops, certain qualities that are not reducible to the component parts that make up our brain emerge. In answer to the question "where does the soul come in?" Ward asserts, "The conclusion must be that the soul is generated by a particular physical system. At a specific point in time, a subject of rational consciousness comes into being. All conscious states belong to a subject, which is able to understand, deliberate, formulate goals and initiate actions."[39]

Now, for Christians, a key capacity of the soul is to engage with the transcendent, but it also includes the capacity for awareness, decision, intention, agency, and some form of moral deliberation. It is not at all a ghost in the machine. It is neither a ghost (some invisible entity) nor a machine (something that is a self-determined system of cause and effect). Instead the soul (or mind) is made possible by the complexity of the brain, which importantly enables the mind to exercise free will and agency.

The key step in this account of personhood is that soul in this world (there could be other worlds where soul would not need to take this particular form) arises as a result of the complexity of the brain, due to "top-down causation" resulting in consciousness. Keith Ward writes:

> It follows from what I have been saying that we could, in theory, make artificial intelligence machines, super-computers, which really would have souls. That is, they would have states of conscious understanding, freedom and moral responsibility, and relationship to God.... In fact, I do not see why we should deny that possibility. We bring souls into existence whenever we have children. We can now fertilize embryos in laboratories, so that our control over procreation is increasing. It is possible, in theory, to construct a genetic sequence, which will begin embryonic development and so create a human life artificially. It is not out of the question that we could also construct a replica of such sequences in other forms, and so create quite new sorts of souls.[40]

Ward's point is simple: humans already create "souls" when we have children. And with advancements around reproductive treatments, we can "clone" and provide "IVF" (In Vitro fertilization), which is a new way of producing souls. So perhaps those at the cutting edge of AI are also in the remarkable and holy work of making souls.

---

39. Ward, *The Battle for the Soul*, 139–40.
40. Ward, *The Battle for the Soul*, 143.

Here is Ward at his most speculative. He is not afraid to follow all the way to a startling conclusion. Given this view of personhood, given the relationship in this world between the material and mind, given the ways in which humans already create persons, then it is possible that technology will find a way to generate consciousness.

STANDING BACK

Let us start by summarizing the main features of Keith Ward's approach to theology:

1. It is committed to the possibility of providing a theological account that is coherent and has explanatory power.
2. It is global in its scope and takes seriously the insights of other religious traditions.
3. It is committed to engage with truth in science; and it is willing to link to a certain scientific approach, even if this runs the risk that the scientific model will be superseded.
4. It takes seriously the doctrinal claims of the church, affirming the virgin birth and holding a high view of the sacraments.
5. It is willing to follow an argument through to a logical possibility and therefore speculate beyond what can be reasonably known.

Now, this approach to theology has its detractors. Gordon Kaufman would be front and central. Keith Ward is not taking seriously the deep injustice that shapes our world. He is not recognizing the ways in which theology can often support oppression.

I do feel that many of these identity theologies have an important insight. The persistence of patriarchy, homophobia, and racism is deep and constant. At Virginia Theological Seminary, I am persuaded that the almost subconscious impact of art in Scott Lounge or plaques in chapel did maintain a culture of whiteness and prejudice. Even though the community was overwhelmingly "liberal" in outlook, the blindness and insensitivity of the environment continued to make the study here for persons of color very difficult. Therefore, it seems to be very likely that how we speak of God might have certain unintended consequences of reinforcing prejudice and injustice.

Nevertheless, I do want to endorse the Ward methodology. My problem with Kaufman is that his very attractive justice-oriented symbol system for God and Christ has zero connection with the truth about what God and Christ might really be about. In other words, precisely because Kaufman feels that the truth is inaccessible and the task of theology is exclusively focused on relating religious language to life, he cannot claim that *in reality* God is opposed to injustice. He cannot claim this because the work of theology is just a language work; it is nothing to do with reality.

Keith Ward's approach is interested in *reality*. The God of Keith Ward really exists. The scientific narrative is suggested of the reality of that God. This is a God that is not Eurocentric because other religious traditions need to be taken seriously. This is a God that redeems animals and may require us to baptize computers. And this God really does think that injustice is an evil and must be confronted by all people in every way they can.

It is ironic. So many advocates of the ordination of women and LGBT+ clergy do so on a theology that is agnostic, tentative, unsure, and projection. The achievement of Keith Ward is that he advocates for the ordination of women and LGBT+ clergy because he really thinks God exists and that there are an abundance of reasons for their inclusion. Keith Ward might be unfashionable; but he is right.

BIBLIOGRAPHY

Conway Morris, Simon. *Life's Solution: Inevitable Humans in a Lonely Universe*. Cambridge: Cambridge University Press, 2003.

Jantzen, Grace. *Becoming Divine: Towards a Feminist Philosophy of Religion*. Manchester: Manchester University Press, 1998.

Jennings, Willie James. *The Christian Imagination: Theology and the Origins of Race*. New Haven, CT: Yale University Press, 2010.

Kaufman, Gordon D. *In Face of Mystery: A Constructive Theology*. Cambridge: Harvard University Press, 1993

Markham, Ian S. "The Plugged-in Church: Is It Appropriate to Baptize Artificial Intelligence." In *The Craft of Innovative Theology: Argument and Process*, edited by John Allan Knight and Ian S. Markham, 50–63. Hoboken, NJ: Wiley, 2022.

———. *A Theology of Engagement*. Oxford: Wiley, 2003.

———. *Understanding Christian Doctrine*. Oxford: Wiley, 2017.

Ward, Keith. *The Battle for the Soul: An Affirmation of Human Dignity and Value*. London: Hodder and Stoughton, 1985.

———. *Christ and the Cosmos: A Reformulation of Trinitarian Doctrine*. Cambridge: Cambridge University Press, 2015.

———. *God, Faith and the New Millennium: Christian Belief in an Age of Science.* Oxford: Oxford University Press, 1998.
———. *Rational Theology and the Creativity of God.* Cleveland, OH: Pilgrim, 1982.
———. *Religion and Community.* Oxford: Clarendon, 2000.
———. *Religion and Creation.* Oxford: Clarendon, 1996.
———. *Religion and Revelation.* Oxford: Clarendon, 1994.
———. *A Vision to Pursue: Beyond the Crisis in Christianity.* London: SCM, 1991.

Keith Ward's Response to Ian S. Markham

IF THE PRESIDENT OF the Virginia Theological Seminary says that I am right, I should really just say "thank you very much" and move on. But I will say something about my methodology in theology. It results from the fact that I was trained in philosophy, and taught it for many years—in fact, until I was eighty-one—in various British universities. I taught it when I would not have called myself a Christian, though I became a Christian priest at the age of thirty-two, when I was teaching philosophy at King's College London. This was partly due to my having what I believed to be an experience of Jesus Christ, a vivid and life-changing experience. And it was partly because my philosophical views increasingly led me toward a Christian view of the world.

The British tradition in philosophy, epitomized by Locke, Berkeley, and Hume, was empiricist. That meant it insisted that all human knowledge begins with "ideas"—sense-perceptions, sensations, feelings, and thoughts. Many empiricists are atheists—A. J. Ayer being the best known modern example. That is because they think there can be no perceptions of God. Since I thought I had encountered Christ, I could not agree. I preferred Berkeley's view that all ideas are in minds, that humans receive their ideas from outside themselves, and therefore that there is a supreme Mind where all possible ideas reside. I quite quickly became an idealist, a philosopher who thinks that the ultimate reality is the cosmic Mind, and the whole physical universe is an expression of Mind.

I was ready for Christianity, but I came to it from an odd place, a place that Karl Barth, for example, derided as arbitrary and willful. This has made me slightly odd among many modern theologians. Idealist philosophy never seemed to me arbitrary and willful. It was not looking for a God who could make all things alright in the end, or who was some sort of symbol for social justice. It was looking for the most consistent, coherent, adequate, and explanatory account of this mysterious and wonderful universe. So of course it had to take science very seriously, since science has completely transformed our view of the universe in the last few centuries.

And it had to take logic, the basic rules of logical discourse, seriously. Mathematical logic was a subject I taught, and logic and mathematics are not in any way culturally relative or supportive of social injustice. Logic simply provides rules for talking sense, but it is a purely formal subject. It does not tell anyone what to think. It just tells people how not to contradict themselves or talk nonsense. If you put nonsense into a formal argument, you will get nonsense out, but at least it will be logical nonsense. This, of course, is why very logical people still disagree. They start with different premises, and logic does not tell you which premises are true.

As an idealist, I had to find some way of finding scientifically informed and logically robust reasons for my philosophy, since many philosophers did not agree with me. Quite a lot of philosophers are materialists, who do not even think that minds exist. But philosophers like disagreeing, and hold their beliefs with conviction, while being aware that other philosophers have good reasons for their beliefs, and are usually neither willful nor arbitrary.

However, I came to find theology even more interesting than philosophy, and became a theologian. But I took my philosophical baggage with me, and tried to find a scientifically informed, logically coherent, and rationally defensible (not strictly provable, except to me and my friends) form of Christian faith. This meant knowing and respecting, but not blindly obeying, the main traditions of Christianity. It also meant looking at a whole range of religious views that were potentially compatible with idealism, to be sure that I had not missed anything—that is certainly necessary to forming a defensible view

That is my methodology, as Ian rightly says. It is opposed to any view, like that of Barth, that refuses to allow critical reason any part to play in constructing religious ideas. (Of course they are constructed; but, like mathematical ideas, they are meant to be true.) And it is opposed to any idea that they are to be assessed by whether they support a program of social justice. For it is sadly true that some fervent supporters of social justice are just wrong about the facts and about the best way to achieve a just society.

I should be clear that an idealist will almost always say that the cosmic Mind is also the supreme Value, so it will in fact support universal justice and compassion for all sentient beings. But what really matters is whether there are objective (not just invented) values of truth and goodness that are demanding. Only if something like Christian idealism is true can anyone ground a realistic hope that self-giving love will triumph over evil, and can promise judgment on those who fail to show such love. Social justice is important, but the striving for it must be grounded on a truth, on the objective reality and efficacy of goodness. That is what theology, supported by philosophical enquiry, can and should provide.

DISCUSSION QUESTIONS

1. List the five main features of Keith Ward's approach to theology.
2. Compare and contrast how Ward and Kaufman approach the intersection of Christian theology and social justice.
3. A sympathetic reader concludes that Ward's "critical realistic" view of reality leads him to a more intellectually robust Christianity, constructed not merely by cultural influences but grounded in timeless rationality and logic. Do you agree? Why or why not?
4. Does Ward's "open theology" stand in tension with orthodox Christianity? Why or why not?
5. How does Ward incorporate the latest scientific insights (for example, interpretations of quantum mechanics) into his theistic worldview? What are possible risks or benefits to aligning one's theology with a particular scientific interpretation?
6. How might Ward's methodological approach to answering questions about extraterrestrial life, animal immortality, and artificial intelligence differ from that of a different contemporary theologian?

2

Probing Ward's Personal Idealism

Faith, Foundation, or Regulative Ideal?

PHILIP CLAYTON AND JAEHA WOO

THE TASK AT HAND

The heart of Keith Ward's personal idealism (PI) is the claim that there is a primordial creative Mind with "ontological and causal priority" in the universe—the personal being many call God.[1] Throughout *The Christian Idea of God*, he argues for PI as the metaphysical framework that can serve as "a strong *philosophical foundation* for Christian belief."[2] Because the book is meant to succeed both as "a work of philosophy" and "a work of Christian theology,"[3] it includes both a philosophical case for PI and an explanation of how that view supports Christian belief. Although Ward does not think of PI as a position that can be established with "absolute theoretical certainty,"[4] he often makes very strong statements on behalf of his view, such as the following: "this postulate . . . is the *most adequate available philosophical description of the nature of reality*."[5]

---

1. Ward, *The Christian Idea of God*, 11.
2. Ward, *The Christian Idea of God*, 1 (emphasis added). Cf. Ward, *The Christian Idea of God*, 221. "It seems to me that a personal idealism provides a sound rational and reflective *basis* for" Christian faith.
3. Ward, *The Christian Idea of God*, 1.
4. Ward, *The Christian Idea of God*, 14.
5. Ward, *The Christian Idea of God*, 213 (emphasis added).

The status of Ward's claims is puzzling, however. *Sometimes* he presents PI as the best available philosophical description of the nature of reality; at other times he describes it as a *postulate* or an *interpretative hypothesis*, two terms that he often uses interchangeably.[6] As he puts it, PI interprets "some experienced reality in terms of concepts that do not derive simply from the observations in themselves."[7] Ward acknowledges that many will not be satisfied with treating God as a postulate, but he thinks that pointing out the practical benefits of adopting this postulate should be enough to counteract this worry. This may also explain why he regularly connects PI as a philosophical position to the experiences of revelation that are often reported by Jews, Christians, and Muslims.

In most of Ward's writings, it certainly *appears* that he is claiming to establish PI as the best available metaphysical hypothesis. And yet ambiguities quickly arise. He reminds us that "God is not a scientific hypothesis."[8] Fair enough. To our knowledge Ward never speaks of God as an explanatory hypothesis, such that one could apply the criteria for "inference to the best explanation" in deciding among the competing explanatory options.[9] Instead, he frequently writes that metaphysics involves "interpretative hypotheses." Can interpretative hypotheses really be evaluated through objective arguments of the sort that metaphysicians love, or do they depend upon irreducibly subjective or communal judgments, as in the *Verstehen* tradition of Wilhelm Dilthey, the sociology of Peter Winch, or the epistemology of the later Wittgenstein? Are there any common criteria for these interpretative hypotheses, or do some people's subjective experiences (say, their religious experiences) justify them to infer certain conclusions that people who lack those experiences are *not* justified in inferring?

Given the ambiguities that run through Ward's writing on these issues, a central question drives our inquiry: How serious is Ward's investment in defending PI as the philosophical foundation for the Christian faith? This guiding question has two components. First, is Ward ready to stake everything on the claim that *personal* idealism is philosophically superior to its

---

6. Cf. Ward, *The Christian Idea of God*, 55. "I will try to show that the idea of God is a reasonable and natural interpretative hypothesis that helps us integrate these [the physical world, beauty, morality, and personal presence] into a coherent whole.... [T]he postulate of something like God helps make sense of the wider range of human experience."

7. Ward, *The Christian Idea of God*, 52. See the explanation of the distinction between two kinds of explanatory hypothesis (interpretative vs. inferential) in 51–54.

8. Ward, *Is Religion Irrational?*, 10.

9. Lipton, *Inference to the Best Explanation*.

closest contenders? Or, when push comes to shove, would he default to defending a more generic idealism as long as it wins out over "materialism," his *bête noire*? And second, is metaphysical adequacy really Ward's final goal? Does he really intend to stake the entire match on a fully *philosophical* defense—*viz.*, PI wins the metaphysical battle on philosophical criteria alone—as opposed to less rigorous epistemic standards, which might include establishing PI as a reasonable assumption, an allowable resting place for those whose faith seeks understanding, a Kantian postulate, or a useful fiction?[10]

DEFINING THE QUESTION

Let's take the first component first. It's in Ward's defense of PI that the major divergence between his methodology and ours begins to emerge. Our approach is to zero in on the closest alternatives, asking whether they are better justified than PI. By contrast, Ward tends to focus on just one or two major alternatives that stand in the sharpest contrast to PI. The major alternative he opposes is "materialism, which claims that everything that exists is a form of matter."[11] Against this position, he carefully argues for postulating the existence of a primordial creative mind. But to this general hypothesis of a cosmic mind he then adds more specific elements, including most notably "the personal characteristics of knowing, feeling, and willing,"[12] which together, he argues, justify the label "personal idealism."[3] But as soon as Ward gives PI a specific form—"knowing, feeling, and willing," for example—a number of other plausible forms of idealism come into view as well, some of which, at least at first blush, appear to be highly attractive and plausible alternative positions. Surely one would have to show why these neighboring idealisms are less adequate before one could proclaim Ward's particular preference to be "the most adequate available philosophical description of the nature of reality."[13]

Consider now the second component, the rich varieties of knowledge claims that one can make . . . or not make. How to order them? If there's to be any hope of clarity, we will argue, surely sharper distinctions have to be

---

10. See Clayton and Knapp, *The Predicament of Belief*, chapter 7, for a list of six epistemic levels (L1–L6). Only L1 and L2 provide a fully philosophical defense.

11. Ward, *The Christian Idea of God*, 1.

12. Ward, *The Christian Idea of God*, 11.

13. Ward, *The Christian Idea of God*, 213.

drawn between metaphysical hypotheses and postulates. A hypothesis is, by definition, a claim to be tested. By contrast, "postulate" can have at least three different senses: (1) God can be postulated as a hypothesis that purports to describe the nature of reality, a hypothesis that one then proceeds to test; (2) God can be postulated as a core assumption, that is, as a premise that cannot be tested but that structures everything that follows; or finally (3) Kant's postulation of God as a regulative principle—a premise that governs "pure" or "practical" reason without making any constitutive claims about the nature of reality—represents a third alternative, as we show below. To run the three senses together, as Ward sometimes does, leaves unclear what argumentative burden he is actually taking on. More worryingly, it leaves the reader unsure what status to ascribe to God language.

We are driven by a question that is at least allied to Ward's interests: what would it take to establish that PI is not just a *possible* "philosophical foundation for Christian belief," but the strongest one? Can one show that PI is philosophically preferable to its nearest competitors? If this task fails, Ward (and we!) need first to admit failure before we transition to some of the less ambitious claims that he makes in his writings.

It is hard, if not impossible, to abandon the metaphysical quest for the most adequate philosophical foundation. Still, at the end of the day, it may be really difficult, if not just about impossible, to establish the objective superiority of one holistic metaphysical system over another. If that possibility is in question, the second (epistemic) critique in our treatment of Keith Ward becomes all the more pressing.

PERSONAL IDEALISM AND DIVINE PERFECTION

Ward's postulate of PI goes beyond affirming the priority of mind over matter. He presents the mind that creates the world and endows it with purpose as not only primordial, but also *perfect*: "nature . . . is not itself supremely perfect by any test," but "God alone is worthy of absolute worship—reverence for that which is without flaw or imperfection."[14] Nature can still be sacred or good, but this sacredness consists "in its capacity to express in many finite forms transcendent divine perfection."[15] Like us, Ward is critical of the traditional tendency to think of perfection as incompatible with change. He does not argue for conceptualizing God as immutable and

14. Ward, *The Christian Idea of God*, 115.
15. Ward, *The Christian Idea of God*, 120.

impassible,[16] but instead thinks of the God of PI as "a progressively self unfolding mind."[17] Still, the fact that Ward makes this point by criticizing the *traditional* understanding of perfection shows that he wants to hold onto the category of perfection when spelling out the idea of God. In this sense, the *language of divine perfection* remains an unmistakable part of Ward's PI.

But why should we think of God as perfect when nature, God's created product, is not? Even if one agrees with Ward that there is "good reason to distance a creator God from nature *if* we are to call God of supreme value, worthy of worship,"[18] why suppose that God is of supreme value and worthy of worship in the first place? This is the question Hume raises in *Dialogues Concerning Natural Religion*,[19] and it is repeated by Kant in the *Critique of Pure Reason*.[20] The question arose in particular as a response to "the design argument, of which William Paley stands as the classic representative. It's worth noting that Ward himself is critical of Paley's view of nature "as the perfect contrivance of a God who designs every detail for the best."[21] But then what is the need to conceive the creative cause of this imperfect nature as perfect? Why call God "a being of supreme knowledge and power"[22] as well as "perfect goodness"?[23] Would it not be more reasonable to think of God as imperfect, in accordance with the imperfections of nature we see?

In *God and the Philosophers*, Ward's response to Hume's critique of the design argument is in part to note that Hume fails to grasp that a "living belief in God is not an inductive inference to an unseen intelligence"; rather, it "is an encounter with a personal reality that transcends all finite experience."[24] It appears that Ward here switches away from making the philosophical case for PI, turning instead to PI's adequacy as a means for describing one's own inner religious experience. If that's the case, let's name the dilemma: in order to answer Hume, it appears, one must either change the hypothesis one is defending, or exit the philosophical arena by making an appeal to religious experience. The former route is taken by Clayton

---

16. Ward, *The Christian Idea of God*, 147.
17. Ward, *The Christian Idea of God*, 133.
18. Ward, *The Christian Idea of God*, 114 (emphasis added).
19. Hume, *Dialogues Concerning Natural Religion*, Part 5.
20. Kant, *Critique of Pure Reason*, A620/B648–A630/B658.
21. Ward, *The Christian Idea of God*, 106.
22. Ward, *The Christian Idea of God*, 128.
23. Ward, *The Christian Idea of God*, 120.
24. Ward, *God and the Philosophers*, 73.

in *The Problem of God in Modern Thought*;[25] it involves the turn from the medieval metaphysics of divine perfection to the philosophical theology of Schelling and Whitehead. The latter route is taken, for example, in the *fides quaerens intellectum* tradition, where one postulates the truth of one's faith and seeks ways to understand it.

It at least appears that Ward wishes to march down both roads at the same time. He does give weight to the encounter with a personal reality. But he also insists that the "God hypothesis is put forward as the most compelling integrating postulate that provides a rational interpretative scheme for all the diverse forms of human experience," including "apprehensions of transcendent value and life-transforming intimations of human fulfillment."[26] He is right, of course, that the reality addressed by a theistic hypothesis cannot be confined to "sense experience." But the question of why all these dimensions of human experience require one to postulate divine perfection still remains. Even if we suppose that what we experience as objective values in the world are such because they are both apprehended and intended as the goals of the cosmos by the primordial Mind, do we have to think of these values as *perfectly instantiated in this Mind*?[27]

In *Morality, Autonomy, and God*, Ward explains his answer to this question by appealing to God's rationality.[28] Because God chooses to actualize one possible initial state of the world over many other possible states,

---

25. Clayton, *The Problem of God in Modern Thought*.
26. Ward, *God and the Philosophers*, 74.
27. Cf. Ward, *God and the Philosophers*, 69.

28. A similar argument is found in the following passage of Ward, *Is Religion Irrational?*, 28. Quotation: "But why is God perfectly good, for Aristotle? Because God is perfectly intelligible, so there must be a good reason for God's existence. One reason is that God is necessary. God cannot fail to exist—and that is a very good reason for existing. But there is another reason. If God is anything like a mind, the best reason for a mind to choose something is that it is good. So the best reason for a mind to exist is that it realizes in itself the best possible sorts of goodness. . . . God wills God to exist, even though God cannot change or cease to be. For God is the most worthwhile thing that could ever exist. God is, as Plato put it, "goodness itself," the standard of perfection, realizing in his own being the highest forms of goodness and beauty. This is what any rational mind would choose for itself if it could. The basic metaphysical (not scientific) hypothesis is that God exists for the best possible reason. And the best possible reason is that the existence of God is supremely worthwhile, just for its own sake. A perfectly rational mind would therefore choose for itself, or realize in itself, the highest possible goods, or set of intrinsically worthwhile states."

Contrast this with the following line in Ward, *The Christian Idea of God*, 128. Quotation: "An eternal mind could not . . . choose its own nature, or the primordial list of possible things that it knows."

God has to be a "mind that can act for a reason."[29] Since "all rational beings will, other things being equal, aim at . . . what is good for them . . . God will instantiate in the divine being the highest set of values that could possibly exist."[30] But this answer seems to assume that God has the requisite power and knowledge to instantiate these values to the fullest,[31] which is precisely part of what Hume questions. Also, can we establish that the being of God is solely constituted by a rationality that chooses to instantiate objective values? Or is it possible that other factors are at play that interfere with, or perhaps even trump, pure rationality?

At several points in *The Christian Idea of God* when it becomes appropriate to address these questions, Ward points out that divine perfection and its cognate ideas are what many religious practitioners commonly believe. He notes, for instance, that "Christians have usually supposed, and are logically obliged to suppose, that . . . God . . . is supremely rational and . . . supremely good."[32] He also speaks of "a widely accepted idea that the nature of ultimate reality is an eternal mind of supreme beauty, wisdom, and bliss."[33] But surely it would be circular to base PI on Christian premises, and then to proceed to use PI as the *foundation* for specifically Christian beliefs. In Ward's use of the notion of divine perfection, it at least appears that this sort of circularity is at play.

Now perhaps Ward had specifically Christian ideas in mind when he constructed PI, filling out its contents by distilling Christian and other religious ideas into the form of a cosmological and metaphysical theory.[34] But if Christian beliefs played a role in the genesis of his metaphysical theory, he cannot *argue for* that theory by appealing to these specifically religious ideas, because this would make his major claim that "there is a natural

---

29. Ward, *The Christian Idea of God*, 98.
30. Ward, *Morality, Autonomy, and God*, 108.
31. For example, Ward, *Morality, Autonomy, and God*, 108. Quotation: "For God not only knows all possibles. God also knows, in the fullest, richest, and most intimate and intense way, every actual form of good that ever exists."
32. Ward, *The Christian Idea of God*, 70.
33. Ward, *The Christian Idea of God*, 129.
34. In Ward, *The Christian Idea of God*, 179, Ward admits, "it would be disingenuous of me to pretend that the Christian tradition (in large part shared by Jews, Muslims, and many Hindus) has played no part in my speculations." "Speculations" here refers to his thoughts regarding the afterlife, but perhaps the same can be said for the more fundamental parts of personal idealism.

affinity between Christianity and personal idealism" wholly unremarkable.[35] One needs an independent argument for treating the primordial Mind as free of imperfections. For example, Andrew Davis has developed something like this argument in his recent book. Is the same true of Ward?

We close with a related concern: The God of PI not only is perfect, but also relates to the created world in certain ways. As Ward notes, "the supreme mind may indeed create an environment to which it can relate and together with which it can in some sense develop."[36] But even if one grants that God *may* act in this way, what is the positive reason for including this element in a metaphysical theory? More specifically, Ward adds that God's relation to the world involves the work of "reinforc[ing] good tendencies and imped[ing] bad ones" in order to "achieve a state of unique beauty and goodness,"[37] a process that, he affirms, culminates in "conscious union with the supreme self."[38] But even if we think of God as the one who intends objective goods in the created world, how does Ward establish that God *actively promotes* realization of these goods by finite minds, and why does this divine activity involve personal relation culminating in conscious union? Even if we assume that personal relationships are an objective value in the world, do we have to think of God as instantiating this value in the God-world relation to explain this objectivity, especially if divine perfection is questionable?[39] Here, again, it appears that an appeal to the Christian tradition of a providential God who acts in the world serves as the implicit

---

35. Ward, *The Christian Idea of God*, 221. In the beginning part of Part III of *The Christian Idea of God*, Ward describes this part as his discussion of "another aspect of the supreme mind: its nature as supreme value," which "will enable [him] to show how the rather abstract notion of a necessary ground of being broadens out into the idea of a personal reality," even though his talk of divine perfection starts in Part II. Ward, *The Christian Idea of God*, 141. (His suggestion of "distanc[ing] a creator God from nature if we are to call God of supreme value, worthy of worship" is in Part II as well. Ward, *The Christian Idea of God*, 114.) At this point, it is worth noting his admission that Part III "will be more explicitly Christian, and it will draw much of its material from Christian tradition." Ward, *The Christian Idea of God*, 142. This admission should make us question what kind of warrant is available for including the affirmation of God as supreme value in PI.

36. Ward, *The Christian Idea of God*, 126.

37. Ward, *The Christian Idea of God*, 132.

38. Ward, *The Christian Idea of God*, 134.

39. "If and when God creates other things, the highest form of fulfillment for these beings will be attained by a form of mutually reinforcing relationship that may be called 'loving communion.' . . . God's perfection may express itself . . . in self-giving love." Ward, *Morality, Autonomy, and God*, 108.

justification of PI, which stands in some tension to the stated goal of providing a philosophical foundation for Christian faith.[40]

ON PERSONAL INFINITE MIND, OR: HOW PERSONAL?

Perhaps no quality ascribed to God better illustrates the methodology of comparative metaphysics than the attribute of *personal* or person-like.

Describing God as "a person" represents the one end of the spectrum, followed closely by God as "a personal being." We know of no passage where Ward falls into a crude anthropomorphism of this type. In fact, at one point in *The Christian Idea of God* he guards against treating God as too similar to a human mind.[41] Still, one has to classify Ward's position in this book as *strong personal idealism*. Among other strongly personal attributions, he thinks of the primordial Mind as having the characteristics of knowing, thinking, feeling, and intending.

Theologians and philosophers of religion have found countless ways to nuance the attribution of personal qualities to God. Thomas Aquinas affirms that personal qualities are only analogies, neither equivocal on the one hand nor univocal on the other. Clayton and Knapp argue that, although God is not a personal being, God cannot be *less* than personal; one might label this position not-less-than-personal idealism.[42] In an earlier writing, Ward expressed his endorsement of Richard Swinburne's description of God as "the personal ground of being."[43] Wesley Wildman holds that God transcends the distinction between personal and nonpersonal altogether (and also, incidentally, the distinction between good and bad).

But is it even consistent to affirm personal qualities of an infinite divine being? In the so-called *Atheismusstreit* of 1799, Fichte argued that personhood requires a relationship with other persons. But by definition an infinite being could not be limited by another outside itself; hence an infinite being could not be personal. Paul Tillich well understood the force of this argument, which played a major role in his turn to the Ultimate as infinite in his 1952 book *The Courage to Be,* and which led finally to his turn to the Ground of Being and the language of "Gott über Gott," or

---

40. Cf. Ward, *Morality, Autonomy, and God,* 65–68.
41. Ward, *The Christian Idea of God,* 125–26.
42. Clayton and Knapp, *The Predicament of Belief,* chapter 4.
43. Ward, *God: A Guide for the Perplexed,* 230.

"der Gott über dem Gott des Theismus."[44] It should be noted that Ward actually traces Swinburne's phrase "the personal ground of being" back to Tillich, even though this influence is not pronounced in Ward's argument for PI. There are myriad ways to draw back from the literal affirmation of divine personhood. On (roughly) one end of the continuum, Geoffrey Wainwright interpreted all language about the personal God as true but "doxological," while on the other end the great Jewish philosopher Maimonides (Rambam) insisted that *no* positive predicate ascribed to God is true; anthropomorphic qualities in particular, like personhood, must be treated as metaphors.

On this question, the Vedantic philosophers in the Hindu tradition have navigated the boundary between the sayable and the unsayable with exquisite subtlety and insight. The early twelfth-century philosopher Ramanuja qualified the nondualist position of his great predecessor, Shankara, in order to affirm the personal nature of the Ultimate, Brahman, and to retain some distinction between Atman (soul) and Brahman, though without falling into dualism. Ramanuja was arguably the greatest, and certainly the most nuanced defender of what we now call panentheism in the global history of philosophy. Shankara, by contrast, defending an absolute nondualism (*advaita Vedanta*), affirmed Brahman "without qualities" (*nirguna Brahman*). If Spinoza was the greatest pantheist in the history of Western philosophy, one must acknowledge Shankara as the greatest pantheist in the South Asian tradition. (Ward has argued, by contrast, that Shankara should be classified as a panentheist.)[45] And yet Shankara insists that Brahman-without-qualities must still be understood as *Satcitananda*—being, consciousness, and bliss. Remarkably, two of the qualities still retained in this highly rarefied view of Ultimate Being are ones that we associate with personal being. Even at the boundaries of language, it appears, the drive toward a not-less-than-personal idealism of the Ultimate remains.

INTERIM ASSESSMENT

Inspired by Ward's declaration that he is seeking "the most adequate available philosophical description of the nature of reality,"[46] in the previous section we explored a range of idealisms, running along the spectrum from

---

44. Tillich, *Der Mut zum Sein*, 127.
45. Personal communication. But see Gilead, "Why Spinoza Was Not a Panentheist."
46. Ward, *The Christian Idea of God*, 213.

the most literalistic "God is a person" to the most subtle and nuanced forms of not-less-than-personal idealism. So far we have evaluated each hypothesis on philosophical criteria, without presupposing a particular religious location or pre-commitment. One finds affirmations by Ward that seem to locate him at multiple points along this personalist continuum. Even for his clearest affirmations—for example, that God knows, thinks, feels, and intends—it is often unclear why one should affirm this particular form of PI and not a close alternative.

We now turn from the first component of our analysis (the particular metaphysical position one advances) to the second component (the status one claims for one's conclusions). This second perspective is essential because, as noted earlier, Ward's writings provide ample evidence that he has other interests than philosophy. There is nothing contradictory should Ward wish to affirm something like the following: "My initial hope was to demonstrate that PI outperforms all other contenders as the best available philosophical description of reality. Still, even if I failed to decisively establish that conclusion, I *was* able to show that PI is a consistent position and to refute some of the standard objections against it." For example, one could argue instead that PI is the metaphysical view that best expresses one's personal experience of the risen Christ, or the view that accords most closely with the Nicene Creed. Following Cornelius van Til, one could even treat one's entire metaphysical position as a pure postulate ("metaphysical presuppositionalism"). Our point is only that one must be clear about what one is claiming to have established.

So how *can* religious believers find a form of rigorous reflection that allows them to ascribe a special status to the beliefs that they hold dear, without having to fall back to the more neutral standards of philosophical rationality? If we are right that Ward's particular version of PI does not clearly win out over all other varieties of idealism in a metaphysical head-to-head combat, what *other* considerations can believers appeal to as they seek to justify adopting a specific understanding of God? Among all the varieties of postulates that don't purport to offer a metaphysical ("constitutive") description of reality, Kantian postulates represent a particularly ingenious attempt to support affirmations about God that may be impossible to establish through metaphysical argumentation.

POSTULATING GOD THE KANTIAN WAY

Kant defends affirming the existence of God as a practical postulate through his moral argument, which Ward explicitly endorses at one point.[47] Even though elements of Kant's argument are found among other forms of idealism, the unique way that Kant orders the elements is particularly compelling. Admittedly, Kant offers different versions of his moral argument as he continues to tinker with it across his three Critiques. Still, in each case he affirms the highest good—the state of perfect distributive justice for all humans in the world—early in the argument. This state of affairs, Kant argues, is the goal of any morality that we might wish to postulate as a possibility. Because Kant (correctly) recognizes that the world at present lacks this perfect justice, he is led to two postulates as the conditions of the possibility of having the highest good realized: the existence of God and the afterlife. These two postulates, with all the requisite attributes for bringing about the highest good, *follow from* the affirmation of a future highest good as a possibility.

Note that the general flow of Kant's argument moves in the opposite direction from Ward's *The Christian Idea of God*. Ward first attempts to establish his view of God, the primordial and supreme Mind, as the best established metaphysical theory, and *then* appeals to it as the basis for his speculations on the afterlife and "the full realization" of distinctive values in the world[48]—which is the functional equivalent for him to the highest good in Kant's system.[49] For Ward, the full realization of values is the highest hope we can entertain based on his idea of God, although he stops short of claiming that God definitely will bring this about.

By contrast, Kant's postulate of God is informed by his idea of the highest good, which he does not claim to be a present reality. As a result, Kant's postulate is bound to be different from Ward's use of the term postulate as an interpretative hypothesis, which aims to provide the most adequate description of reality we experience *at present*. Of course, the idea of the highest good is not completely disconnected from the present reality, even for Kant. After all, he is led to the highest good by identifying the

---

47. Ward, *The Christian Idea of God*, 168n. See also Ward, *Morality, Autonomy, and God*, 119–28.

48. Ward, *The Christian Idea of God*, 159.

49. Admittedly, there are brief mentions of hope for the full realization of these values in Ward's argument for treating the primordial mind as supreme and perfect. For instance, see Ward, *The Christian Idea of God*, 61.

(present) sense that morality aims at this goal. In fact, the most common form of his moral argument even suggests that actualizing this goal is a necessary demand of the moral law, and he would treat this demand as a bit of experience everyone shares in principle. Interestingly, this is exactly the kind of moral experience that Ward especially stresses when he presents PI as a plausible hypothesis. But Kant is much more clear that the idea of the highest good contrasts with reality as we know it at present, as the following passage in the third *Critique* suggests:

> As soon as human beings began to reflect on right and wrong, at a time when they still indifferently looked over the purposiveness of nature, ... the judgment must inevitably have occurred to them that it could not in the end make no difference if a person has conducted himself honestly or falsely, fairly or violently, *even if* to the end of his life he has found at least *no visible reward* for his virtues *or punishment* for his crimes. It is as if they heard an *inner voice that things must come out differently* .... [50]

According to Kant, the present evidence suggests that rewards and punishments do not always match our virtues and crimes—hence the lack of perfect distributive justice in the present world, where too often morally evil people seem to prosper while undeserved sufferings abound. But the inner voice must still protest against this evidence and postulate a different order of the world: the order of the highest good, in which present injustices will be properly addressed in the afterlife through God's agency.

In *An Enquiry Concerning Human Understanding*, Hume raises the following question, which is very similar in spirit to his question (discussed above) about how the design argument can establish divine perfection: if the present world lacks perfect distributive justice, why suppose that it will be achieved "beyond the ordinary course of events"?[51] The point is that, if we deduce causes only from effects, this kind of supposition seems unjustified, since it is derived not from our observation of effects but from our "own conceit and imagination."[52] This is precisely the point where Kant seeks to overcome Hume's skepticism. It may well be that our standard application of induction leads us to posit a future that is essentially similar to the present reality. According to Kant, however, practical considerations make it crucial to imagine a future with an order different from the present

---

50. Kant, *Critique of the Power of Judgment*, 5:458 (emphasis added).
51. Hume, *An Enquiry Concerning Human Understanding*, 193.
52. Hume, *An Enquiry Concerning Human Understanding*, 193.

one. Indeed, Kant treats this imagination of perfect justice in the future as the more adequate basis from which to derive the attributes of divine perfection affirmed in the classical conception of God than the present imperfect reality. This explains why Kant favors the moral argument over the design argument, insofar as "*moral* teleology makes good the defect of *physical* teleology, and first establishes a *theology*."[53] In short, what determines the details of the concept of God as a postulate in Kant's system is the highest good as a vision of future, and *not* a hypothesis about the best available explanation of the present reality.[54]

THE PLACE OF HOPE IN A PHILOSOPHICAL FOUNDATION FOR RELIGIOUS FAITH

Although Kant often describes the highest good as an idea that is subjectively necessary for all humans, critics of his moral argument have often claimed that he failed to establish this conclusion. This is also Ward's assessment as, for example, when he notes that "we must rein in [Kant's] universalistic claim a little."[55] But even if the claim of *universal subjective necessity* goes too far, one can still regard it as *a hope we may entertain*, and this represents Ward's attitude toward the highest good or full realization of values in the future. If so, what Kant's moral argument suggests is that the attitude of hope may come into play in the early stages of arguing for the details of the idea of God. Even though Ward is eager to point out the practical benefits of such a future-oriented hope, he seems reluctant to admit how much his particular idea of God may be grounded in hope. Instead, his intention is to provide "moral commitment and moral hope" with "a firm metaphysical foundation in [his] philosophy" of PI.[56] We doubt, however,

---

53. Kant, *Critique of the Power of Judgment*, 5:444.

54. Another reason why Kant prefers his moral argument to physical teleology is that the former purports to establish the postulate of God with necessity, which an interpretative hypothesis cannot dare to claim. Because failure to postulate the existence of God who will ensure the highest good in future implies our inevitable failure to achieve the shared end of morality, he thinks this postulate is subjectively necessary for all humans, who are endowed with respect for the moral law. So this postulate becomes a necessary condition of possibility for maintaining morality as an intelligible project. Thus, as the foundation for a theistic faith, his postulate of God is presented as an alternative that outperforms the approach of finding a metaphysical hypothesis as the basis.

55. Ward, *Morality, Autonomy, and God*, 126.

56. Ward, *The Christian Idea of God*, 158.

that he can objectively defend his metaphysical position without grounding it first in hope.

A more Kantian approach would be to assign a more foundational role to this future-oriented hope. As Clayton and Knapp argue in a forthcoming book,[57] perhaps the justification of God language is more *elpidic* (from Greek *elpida*, hope) than *epistemic*. Kant describes the vision of the highest good as a way to overcome "a hindrance to moral resolve,"[58] and Ward recognizes similar practical benefits from hope.[59] Interestingly, Ward connects these practical benefits not just with hope, but also with the choice of idealism over materialism. For instance, he suggests that idealists who hold that "humans will have a part to play in" the purpose set by the primordial mind will end up adopting "a completely different perspective on life from thinking that we are an accidental by-product of a blind and indifferent universe," leading to "huge practical consequences."[60] The idealist option, it appears, has more desirable practical consequences than the materialist one. If positive consequences are part of why some affirm idealism instead of materialism, why can't the positive consequences of adopting a hope-based view play a similar role?

Of course, hoping for something does not make it true. Using language of God in the context of hope is more like a Kantian regulative principle than an argument for God's existence. But Ward has already shown himself to be open to strengths of God-language other than the standard proofs for God's existence and essential attributes. We suggest that the elpidic dimension of God language is an under-developed aspect of Ward's theology.

CONCLUSION

It is easiest to see the shortcomings in those who stand closest to one's own position, and that has certainly been true in these pages. Like Ward, we

---

57. We here anticipate some ideas presented in Clayton and Knapp, *Hope Beyond Belief*.

58. Kant, *Religion Within the Boundaries of Mere Reason*, 6:5.

59. For instance, Ward claims that the Christian vision of the future "world in which the consequences of our life in this world will be justly worked out . . . is not a hope for 'pie in the sky when we die,' which has no implications for our moral and social lives in the World. It is the realization that what we do in this world is of immense importance, because it will determine what our existence in the world to come may be." Ward, *The Christian Idea of God*, 176.

60. Ward, *The Christian Idea of God*, 101.

affirm idealism; and like him, we view personal idealism as the philosophical position that correlates most closely with theism. We are, however, more cautious than he is about apologetics—hence our use of "correlates with" rather than "grounds" in the previous sentence. Also, like Ward, we use God-language in multiple senses: metaphysically, of course, but also regulatively, metaphorically or figuratively, emotively or doxologically, and yes, apophatically.

In these pages we have voiced the call for greater clarity, for sharper arguments on behalf of the particular version(s) of PI that Ward wants to defend, and for more subtle critiques directed at one's neighbors, rather than broadsides directed at one's more distant enemies. Ralph Waldo Emerson may be right that, "A foolish consistency is the hobgoblin of little minds, adored by little statesmen and philosophers and divines. With consistency a great soul has simply nothing to do."[61] Given how demanding is the quest for philosophical foundations, however, precision is not always a bad thing.

Nevertheless, for some thirty years Keith Ward has been taking philosophers, theologians, and scientists on a wild and exciting ride. We would not wish it otherwise.

---

61. Emerson, "Self-Reliance."

BIBLIOGRAPHY

Clayton, Philip. *The Problem of God in Modern Thought*. Grand Rapids: Eerdmans, 2000.

Clayton, Philip, and Steven Knapp. *Hope Beyond Belief: Motivating Action in a Complex World*. Under consideration by Oxford University Press.

———. *The Predicament of Belief: Science, Philosophy, and Faith*. Oxford: Oxford University Press, 2014.

Emerson, Ralph Waldo. "Self-Reliance." In *Essays: First Series*. Boston: James Munroe and Company, 1841.

Gilead, Amihud. "Why Spinoza Was Not a Panentheist." *Philosophia* 49.5 (2021) 2041–51. https://doi.org/10.1007/s11406-021-00378-8.

Hume, David. *Dialogues Concerning Natural Religion*. London: Oxford University Press, 1779.

Hume, David. *An Enquiry Concerning Human Understanding*. Edited by Tom L. Beauchamp. In *Oxford Philosophical Texts*. Oxford: Oxford University Press, 1999.

Kant, Immanuel. *Critique of Pure Reason*. London: Macmillan, 1881.

———. *Critique of the Power of Judgment*. Edited by Paul Guyer, translated by Paul Guyer and Eric Matthews. In *The Cambridge Edition of the Works of Immanuel Kant*. New York: Cambridge University Press, 2000.

———. *Religion Within the Boundaries of Mere Reason*. Cambridge: Cambridge University Press, 1998.

Lipton, Peter. *Inference to the Best Explanation*. London: Routledge, Taylor and Francis, 1994.

Tillich, Paul. *Der Mut zum Sein*. Berlin: de Gruyter, 1952.

Ward, Keith. *The Christian Idea of God: A Philosophical Foundation for Faith*. Cambridge: Cambridge University Press, 2017.

———. *God: A Guide for the Perplexed*. Oxford: Oneworld, 2003.

———. *God and the Philosophers*. London: Augsburg Fortress, 2009.

———. *Is Religion Irrational?* Oxford: SPCK, 2011.

———. *Morality, Autonomy, and God*. London: Oneworld, 2013.

Keith Ward's Response to Philip Clayton and Jaeha Woo

PHILIP CLAYTON'S CRITIQUE OF my view of personal idealism is acute and insightful. Space determines that I can only respond to one of his basic points, by clarifying that when I speak of a postulate, a hypothesis, or a philosophical explanation, I am using different terms for the same thing. Personal idealism postulates the hypothesis that a supreme cosmic Mind, creating a world for the sake of realizing relationships of value between persons, is the best philosophical explanation of how the world is.

It is not, as such, a Christian explanation. But if it is correct, it provides a philosophical foundation for faith, in that it sets out the conditions under which some revelatory experiences of a spiritual reality can occur and are likely to be taken as veridical. Naturally, any such revelations will provide additional content to the general philosophical postulate. But what one thinks revelation shows will in turn be affected by philosophical reflection. The two are not sealed compartments.

For instance, Thomism offers a basically Aristotelian understanding of the universe, which will suggest a particular understanding of a God who is changeless and timeless. Process philosophy will offer a very different understanding, which does not derive from revelation, but which will suggest a rather different understanding of revelation as progressive guidance.

I think personal idealism, while it is not the only account available, and is not a necessary condition of the truth of Christian faith, is the best philosophical account, but views about the nature of revelation (in the life, death, and resurrection of a person) will modify many details of the suggested explanatory scheme. Thus a Christian-revealed belief that all things will be united in Christ will modify an idealist account of the purpose of creation. At the same time, the idealist account might postulate an evolutionary interpretation of this belief that was not in the original revelation. It is in that sense that metaphysical hypotheses and revealed beliefs are not in competition. To take another example, that God suffers may be taken as deriving from Jesus's death on the cross. But it will influence the thought that a God who creates a world containing much evil must share in the experience of that evil—and someone like Whitehead could believe that without being a Christian.

Consideration of suffering in creation may well modify one's understanding of God's perfection. Christian reflection on creaturely freedom might modify accounts of divine omnipotence. This would not mean that Christian beliefs were wrongly inserted into the philosophical foundations of belief. But it might well influence the way one thought about those foundations. Philip asks why a Supreme Mind should be thought of as perfect or infinite. The reason for positing such a Mind is partly to account for the sense of moral demand, and to root it in some objective reality that, as Mind, essentially aims for goodness. In seeking an explanation for the existence of this universe, we want to understand whether there could be a reason for the existence of anything at all. My suggestion is that such a reason has to be axiological. It has to be that the existence of some things is just worthwhile for its own sake. Only if there is something of supreme value can one see that there is an ultimate reason for existence. The postulate of a Mind that is itself of supreme value entails some spelling out of what this value could be. This is where philosophy might wish to replace the ancient Greek values of changeless perfection with more dynamic values of creativity and relationship. Such a God might not be spoken of as infinite or as changelessly perfect. But in seeking Mind as the prior reality, one is also seeking supreme value, and positing that it will lie, not in some impersonal or unconscious reality, but in some form of mental activity.

Philip is seeking such a value-oriented reality when he suggests that a more "elpidic" or hopeful idea ought to be injected into idealist thought (that belief in God might derive from hope) rather than deriving hope for the future from some prior idea of God's perfection. But the postulate of God is precisely founded on the hope that the universe is good, and at the same time that ultimate optimism is not arbitrary, but is founded on a belief that there are reasons for hope, because there is a creator God whose purpose is achievable. The two are mutually reinforcing.

In conclusion, my view is that personal idealism is not the only philosophical foundation for faith. I do think it is the best one. But, as Philip has pointed out with admirable clarity, not everyone is going to agree, and that gives hope that the pilgrimage of thought is by no means at an end.

DISCUSSION QUESTIONS

1. Describe the tension, identified by Clayton and Woo, in that Ward sometimes treats personal idealism as a postulate but other times as an interpretive hypothesis. Does Ward's response resolve this tension?

2. What reasons does Ward give for saying that personal idealism is better than materialism? How does he deal with other kinds of idealism?

3. Do you think Ward's approach convincingly shows that personal idealism is the best choice among these philosophical systems?

4. How does Ward balance giving God personal traits while avoiding anthropomorphism? Compare his approach to that of other philosophers, like Aquinas, Tillich, and Ramanuja.

5. Examine Ward's reasoning for why God, as posited by personal idealism, must be considered perfect despite the imperfections of nature. How does this position respond to classical critiques by philosophers such as Hume and Kant?

6. Kant emphasizes the necessity of imagining a future order of perfect justice. How does this future-oriented hope influence the conception of God in Kant's system, and how does Ward incorporate or differ from this aspect in his own metaphysical framework?

3

Hope Springs Eternal

Grounding a Theology of Divine Hope in the Work of Keith Ward

WM. CURTIS HOLTZEN

According to American Reformed theologian H. Richard Niebuhr, "to ascribe hope to [God] seems too anthropomorphic. . . . So far as I know, the Scriptures never speak of the hope of God though they do speak of his love and faith."[1] It is quite interesting that Niebuhr will attribute to God faith, along with love, but considers hope a step too far. While I believe both faith and hope accent the divine attribute of love, in this essay I will focus on the latter.[2] Hope gives one a reason to act in love. Hope gives an agent motive to take the steps necessary to bring about a desired future.

Niebuhr's claim that divine hope is not biblical is questionable,[3] but his real hurdle to divine hope being too anthropomorphic is tied to his theological sensibilities as a Reformed theologian. What if we step outside that tradition? What if we examine a theology that considers a God who

---

1. Niebuhr, "Reflections on Faith, Hope, and Love," 155. Niebuhr also argues that hope is not possible for God since God transcends time. I will address God, time, and hope later in this essay.

2. For more on faith as a divine attribute see Morgan, *Roman Faith and Christian Faith* and Holtzen, *The God Who Trusts*.

3. David Reimer argues that several places in the Hebrew Bible attest to God's hope. See Reimer "An Overlooked Term in Old Testament Theology: Perhaps."

creatively cooperates with free creatures? For that I turn to the work of Keith Ward.

"God can embrace the suffering which is the result of evil, in the hope of turning the perpetrators of evil to penitence."[4] Here, Keith Ward appears to suggest that God acts in hope. God not only passively hopes that evildoers will turn from their ways by recognizing and accepting salvation, but God actively hopes. God's hope means that God works to "strengthen feeble efforts towards goodness by cooperating in love . . . [to] infuse a knowledge of the divine beauty and perfection in those who are prepared to receive it."[5]

Ward is not alone in speaking of God's hope. Theologians of all stripes have declared, though usually without explanation, God's hope in any number of things. Walter Brueggemann, in discussing God's particular kind of sovereignty, says that "[i]t invites but does not compel. It hopes rather than requires."[6] Concerning prophetic pronouncements of judgment, Terrance Fretheim writes, "it may be said that God hopes that the announcement of judgment will not have to be fulfilled, so that God's salvific will can be realized."[7] What is unique about Ward's theology, however, is that it can *ground* an account of divine hope. Ward's depictions of God as temporally potential, essentially cooperative, creatively powerful, and compassionately loving, in light of his views on human freedom, suggest that God can and should exemplify hope.

While hope is a deeply human trait, it need not be thought of as exclusively a human trait. Hope is a disposition any being with personal qualities could rightly have when facing an open future that is not in their full control. As I explore the work of Professor Ward and use it to ground a theology of divine hope, I am not suggesting that human and divine hope are indistinguishable.

Given God's vast knowledge of both the actual and the potential, God may reasonably have fewer opportunities to hope. However, it may also mean that, because of God's knowledge and power, the hope God exemplifies reveals a perfection that we have not yet dared to imagine.

---

4. Ward, *Religion and Creation*, 264.
5. Ward, *Religion and Creation*, 264.
6. Brueggemann, *Genesis. Interpretation*, 18.
7. Fretheim, "The Repentance of God," 53.

HOPE

The ubiquity of hope is unquestionable. The meaning of hope, however, poses a living question that, in the last few decades, has attracted substantial attention. Probably the most common understanding of hope is a standard desire-belief account. Hope on this view is a combination of desire (attraction) for a certain state or outcome and the belief that said state is possible, but not certain.[8] While this view is common it may be inadequate since it is possible to desire an outcome believed to be possible and yet lack feelings of hope. Also, as Adrianne Martin explains, there are occasions in which a person believes the desired outcome is "extremely improbable" and yet still finds "hope against hope."[9] Furthermore, it seems a person can hope without believing the desired outcome is possible. One can desire some state of affairs but be in doubt[10] about the possibility of that state of affairs. While the standard desire-belief account is widely understood to be inadequate, there is little agreement about just what is missing.

For this essay I will use the standard desire-belief account of hope with four clarifying conditions provided by Aquinas. In explaining why hope is a virtue, Aquinas writes, "Now the act of hope, whereof we speak now, attains God. For, as we have already stated (I-II:40:1), when we were treating of the passion of hope, the object of hope is a future good, difficult but possible to obtain."[11] From this very brief comment Romanus Cessario notes four characteristics of hope. 1) Hope looks to what is good, in our case that is always God. 2) Hope looks toward the future since one never hopes for what she has already obtained. 3) Hope involves some difficulty or arduousness. 4) Hope looks toward what is attainable.[12] While the final characteristic is embedded in the standard desire-belief account, the first three are helpful additions.

If God hopes, it would most certainly be a virtuous hope. According to Aquinas, a virtuous hope looks only for the good, a future good, that is not easily attained but is nonetheless attainable. Can we rightly say that

---

8. As one more philosopher writes, "'A hopes that P' is true if and only if 'A wishes that P, and A thinks that P has some degree of probability, however small' is true" in Day, "Hope," 89.

9. Martin, *Hope We Hope*, 14–17.

10. That is, neither believe that P is possible nor believe that P is not possible.

11. Aquinas, *Summa Theologiae* II-II, Q.17, A.1. Quoted from Kazor, *Thomas Aquinas on Faith, Hope, and Love*.

12. Cessario, "The Theological Virtue of Hope," 232–33.

God desires future goods that are not easily attained but still attainable? As noted below, some would argue it is preposterous to say such things about God. However, I believe Ward's theology of a creatively loving God cooperating with free creatures grounds the claim that hope can most certainly be applied to God.

Philosophical inquiry into the nature of hope typically invites discussion that is not immediately applicable to questions of divine hope. I believe questions concerning the rationality or morality of hope, for example, can be set aside when exploring the hope of a being perfect in wisdom, knowledge, power, and goodness. We need not worry whether God's hope is rational or if God only hopes and works for what is good and beautiful.[13] But if God desires, or is attracted to, some possible state of affairs the actuality of which God cannot wholly guarantee, then it seems right that God does and should hope for that state of affairs.

CLASSICAL THEISM AND DIVINE HOPE

No classical or "mainstream"[14] theists have ever, to my knowledge, developed any kind of theology of divine hope—and a brief overview of classical theism promises to explain why. As noted above, hope involves an agent desiring or being attracted to some future state of affairs and believing this state is possible but is not certain to obtain. Furthermore, virtuous hope is only attracted to good states—and achieving the desired state, because it is arduous, requires perseverance.

Mainstream theology would say God does not experience any state of affairs that God has not freely willed. This is due to God's omnipotent predetermination. As John Calvin said, "[b]y predestination we mean the eternal decree of God, by which he determined with himself whatever he wished to have with regard to every man."[15] Whatever God wills, God alone determines. God is not dependent on any other but the divine self. Logically, God can have no unsatisfied desires because, as John Fienberg writes,

---

13. I am not suggesting that issues of divine motivation, rationality, or ethics are topics unworthy of investigation. I am simply setting them aside as they would be too lengthy for this essay. Here we will assume that God's acts, thoughts, and feelings are perfectly good.

14. Paul Helm prefers the term "mainstream Christian doctrine of God" and believes all other doctrines are deviations from this "main spine of Christian theism." Helm, "Classical Calvinist Doctrine of God," 5–6.

15. Calvin, *Institutes*, 3.21.5.

"God's good pleasure and good purposes determine what he decrees. . . . God has chosen at once the whole interconnected sequence of events and actions that have and will occur in our world."[16] Since God gets whatever God wills there are no states that God hopes for.

Classical theists affirm God's total and perfect omniscience because God has decreed all states and events. For some, this view of absolute divine predestination is too much, especially in light of human freedom, evil, and suffering. Yet, these theists would still affirm God's absolute and perfect knowledge of all events, including future free and contingent events. Exhaustive future foreknowledge entails that even if God does not always get what God wills, God nonetheless is certain of all future states. Roger Olson, who describes himself as a "classical free-will theist," denies that "God is the all-determining reality. . . . [God] does not control or dominate everything creatures do, . . . in order to allow humans limited, situated freedom." However, "God foreknows the entire course of the future as well as its end. . . . Classical free-will theists do not believe this reality robs the future of contingency or freedom."[17] Because hope is only feasible in states in which the agent believes that the desired outcome is possible but not certain, free-will theism, as Olson conceives, has no need or use for a theology of divine hope.

Additional divine attributes, as understood and affirmed by classical theists, such as immutability, impassibility, pure actuality, and simplicity, would also rule out any grounds for a theology of divine hope. It is unnecessary to detail how these additional attributes would diminish a theology of divine hope given that divine timelessness, meticulous omnipotence, and exhaustive future foreknowledge already do so. The classical or mainstream God surely has no use for hope since this God has no unmet desires. But what if the classical idea of God is mistaken? What if God does not have these attributes, at least not in the ways classical theists have defined them? If God's engagement with the world is one of loving cooperation with free beings who make choices God cannot absolutely know before they are made, then it is worth considering a theology of divine hope.

---

16. Feinberg, "God Ordains All Things," 29.
17. Olson, "The Classical Free Will Theist Model of God," 148, 156.

WARD'S PICTURE OF THE DIVINE

Keith Ward's doctrine of God is far too extensive to detail in such a brief work. Thankfully such detail isn't needed. In this section I will briefly set out some of the aspects of Ward's conception of God as they relate to purposes for a dynamic creation and explain how divine hope is not only possible but a logical consequence of just such a conception.

Dual-Aspect of God

Hope is generally thought of as a "uniquely human phenomenon" since animals seem to lack a sense of futurity.[18] What I believe most are suggesting, however, is that hope is a phenomenon unique to persons.[19] Ward, however, says, "Speaking personally, saying 'God *is* a person' is a step too far for me."[20] He gives several reasons for denying that God is a person, one of which regards divine ineffability: "To say that God is ineffable is to say that the essential nature of God, that which is truly definitive of what God is, is beyond the range of any human concepts."[21]

Ward has advanced a dual-aspect conception of God in which God is infinite and finite, eternal and temporal, fully actual and creatively actualizing.[22] God is both indescribable and yet comprehensible. Ward argues that the classical view of God has endured because "It presents the idea of God as infinite being, knowledge and bliss. This divine nature is 'unpierced by evil', impassible and unchanged by the world."[23] Ward affirms Aquinas' view of "Pure Act" meaning that God has "existence in itself, with a necessary and primordial nature beyond all relationship and development. . . . [God

---

18. Waterworth, *A Philosophical Analysis of Hope*, 5. Wittgenstein asks, "One can imagine an animal angry, frightened, unhappy, happy, startled. But hopeful? And why not? A dog believes his master is at the door. But can he also believe his master will come the day after tomorrow?" Wittgenstein, *Philosophical Investigations*, 174.

19. It would be odd to suggest an infant is not a human because it does not experience hope.

20. Ward, *God: A Guide for the Perplexed*, 230.

21. Ward, "Is God a Person?," 70. The other three reasons concern how persons relate to one another and issues concerning the incarnation and the Trinity.

22. Ward, *Concepts of God*, 159.

23. Ward, *Concepts of God*, 155.

is] beyond human comprehension, unlimited, and beyond change, and yet the source of all change and finitude."[24]

If Ward's conception of God ended here, any theology of divine hope would seem to be hopeless. However, Ward argues that God also has an active or expressive nature which "relates to the world in suffering, compassion, and cooperating power."[25] The expressive nature of God "is 'personal' insofar as it holds that the supreme Self has the personal characteristics of knowing, feeling, and willing, even though this being may be much greater than anything we would ordinarily call a 'person.'"[26] To see God as a "person" "is to see God as an Other who encounters us in a personal way, who has a relationship with us which is one of father (or mother) to child, or lover to beloved."[27]

How can one logically affirm these two poles of one God? For Ward it "is to distinguish God in himself from what we can understand of him."[28] The dual-aspect nature of God is mysterious, but it is not a paradox or contradiction.[29] While more could be said on his dual-aspect of God, what is key for this discussion is that God is personal in such a way that divine hope should not immediately be dismissed. God's personal qualities of love, compassion, willing, and cooperation prima facie suggest the inquiry can move forward.

Divine Temporality

As noted above, hope is future oriented. Hope is attraction to some future state that is possible but not certain. I cannot logically hope for what was or what is, since these states are no longer potential but actual. I can still desire that the past or present was other than it is, but this would be a kind of wishing, not hoping.[30] This means that if God is in any sense a hoping

24. Ward, *The Christian Idea of God*, 126.
25. Ward, *The Christian Idea of God*, 133.
26. Ward, *The Christian Idea of God*, 11.
27. Ward, *God: A Guide for the Perplexed*, 231–32.
28. Ward, *The Living God*, 21.
29. Ward, *Sharing in the Divine Nature*, 18.

30. Language allows us to speak of hoping for a past or present state even though we do not logically hope the past or present is other than it is. For example, upon hearing that a friend was involved in a car accident yesterday I might say, "Goodness, I hope she was alright." In this case, I am not thinking that if she was seriously hurt, I am hoping she was not seriously hurt. That makes no sense. I am in a sense hoping that the news of her

Hope Springs Eternal

agent, then God must experience temporality in such a way that the future is genuinely open to possibility.

The biblical writers were not coy in their placement of God "in" time. They speak of God having future plans (Jer 29:11), of God remembering (Exod 2:24), of God having changes of mind (Amos 7:3), and even of God's past, present, and future (Rev 1:4 "Grace to you and peace from him who is and who was and who is to come, and from the seven spirits who are before his throne"). Biblical verses like these alone are surely not sufficient to warrant belief in divine temporality. But such verses show that divine temporality is hardly beyond biblical notions of God.

Keeping in sync with his dual-aspect conception of God, Ward has argued that God is both "timelessly actual" and "temporally potential."[31] "God is an infinite actuality and plenitude of being, changeless and beyond all time and distinction. This same God is also endlessly active, creative and potent for ever-new futures."[32] Even though Ward speaks of God's essence as timeless, he nonetheless eschews notions of time being an artificial category of the divine. In fact, he argues that we can say something analogous to "time exists in God."[33] Furthermore, Ward argues that there are times in which God exists, times God did not create since "he cannot logically create a condition of his own existing. Time becomes a property of God, rather than something he creates."[34]

Time existing in God, or as a property of God, does not mean God experiences time exactly as we do. God is not ravaged by time or overwhelmed by the vastness of the future. God does not grow old and certainly does not forget anything. But it seems reasonable to suggest that our past is God's past and that our future is entailed in God's future. Our timelines run parallel.

The idea of time being a property of God does open vistas for divine hope since time is not merely the condition of a created world. Taking Ward's claim that time in some sense exists in God and that God is the creator of this world, it seems possible that hope has forever been a divine quality, or at least as long as God had planned a creation. For God to make

---

condition, which is still in the future at this point, will be positive. My hope is that the news I will receive is that she is in good health.

31. Ward, *Religion and Creation*, 268.
32. Ward, *Religion and Creation*, 283.
33. Ward, *Sharing in the Divine Nature*, 106.
34. Ward, *Rational Theology and the Creativity of God*, 163.

plans and freely act upon them requires that God experience some sense of temporal duration. "If God is really free in a libertarian sense, then there must be a state in God (presumably a quasi-mental state) at which God is able to do X or Y (to create or not create), followed by a state in which God has chosen X or Y."[35] If state X (to create) has any contingencies, aspects of which God cannot wholly bring about because they include the choices of free creatures, then it seems that for as long as God has desired such a state, and that state has been possible, God has had hopes about that state. Hope then is an authentic potential in God.

Classical theists have maintained that God is timeless because God is perfect and fully actual. A God who experiences the passing of time in any form would be a God less than actual, thus a perfect God must be fully actualized and can have no potential.[36] Ward notes that there is something ironic about such a claim. "[T]here is something incomplete about the concept of a perfect being which is wholly complete, in the sense of being wholly actual, without any potential. For what such a being would lack is precisely potentiality."[37] It is this potentiality that allows God to relate to creatures—cooperate with them, share in their joys and sufferings—but realized potentials require temporality.

Cooperation with free creatures who have a role in the divine plan is where hope would seem most necessary. But I am getting ahead of myself. While temporality is a necessary condition of hope, it is hardly a sufficient condition. Despite what has been said about free creatures, it may simply be the case that God exists temporally but omnipotently controls every moment of the unfolding future. If this is the case, then divine hope is a hopeless venture.

Omnipotence

As stated, even if God experiences the progression of every moment into the next, albeit in ways only analogous to human experiences of time, this alone will not mean God hopes. It may be that God meticulously determines every passing moment, all while God experiences those moments

---

35. Ward, *Sharing in the Divine Nature*, 106.

36. It should be noted that the many times my father told me I had no potential he was not affirming my full actuality and certainly not my perfection.

37. Ward, *Religion and Creation*, 268.

sequentially—a God unlimited in power but situated in time. While this may be the case, this is not how Ward conceives of divine omnipotence.

Ward is critical of claims of absolute or unrestricted divine power since these notions can be self-contradictory. God's power is limited, for example, by God's own nature. "God must have a given nature, which is not chosen, but which God possesses of necessity."[38] Whatever is necessary of God is not under God's power to change. But Ward also affirms that God, as the "greatest possible power cannot be limited in any way by anything other than itself, unless it wills to be, and such limitation will always be under its control."[39] But what if God wills that some creatures have the power to cooperate freely with God, which then necessitates that they can freely reject such cooperation?

Divine omnipotence is most relevant when devising ways to understand how it might work in concert with human freedom. Plainly, if all human thoughts and actions are determined by God (or nature or circumstance) there is little reason for God ever to hope that humans might conform to God's will, since God has either guaranteed that we will or guaranteed that we will not. While Ward speaks of the "completely unresolved question of determinism and freedom" he is nonetheless critical of determinism and compatibilism while affirming a kind of libertarian freedom.[40]

Ward argues that creaturely freedom is necessary for real autonomy. Such autonomous freedom implies that significantly free creatures can and will do things that God does not intend.[41] What God intends is that free creatures finally and fully unite with God and God's perfect goodness. But Ward is clear that even God cannot cause persons to freely unite with God. "The supreme mind has the power to [gradually develop self-organizing entities] but cannot exercise its power coercively without destroying the creative freedom of the emergent order."[42] Furthermore, "if these created minds are really free, they can do things that God does not want them to do.... However, if God wants them to be free, God cannot stop them from being destructive, from doing things God does not want."[43]

---

38. Ward, *Religion and Creation*, 171.
39. Ward, *Religion and Creation*, 167.
40. Ward, *The Big Questions in Science and Religion*, 199.
41. Ward, *God, Chance, and Necessity*, 195.
42. Ward, *The Christian Idea of God*, 133.
43. Ward, *The Christian Idea of God*, 136.

By my lights, Ward's view of human freedom means God desires that we act, feel, and think in certain ways that God, even as a being of maximal power, cannot guarantee. Without some measure of genuine human autonomy, there is little that God would hope for in terms of God's ultimate creational purposes. Everything would be exactly as God willed or as nature determined. A divine omnipotence that allows for, perhaps even necessitates, human freedom is an omnipotence that has the capacity to hope.

Human freedom as such, like divine temporality, does not necessitate a theology of divine hope. In fact, a somewhat popular view is that God has created free creatures that can and do rebel against God's good purposes all while God has eternally known what every free creature would do. If God has been eternally certain of what we will do then this unquestionably invalidates any notion of divine hope.

Omniscience

Divine omniscience is typically defined in terms of God's knowing all truths; and for many theologians, some of those truths include future human free acts. William Lane Craig, for example, claims that God exists in time, allows for human freedom, but also has complete knowledge of what every being will do. While Craig takes a Molinist approach,[44] others assert that God has exhaustive foreknowledge of all future free human acts (and thoughts and feelings) without middle knowledge. This view, commonly known as simple exhaustive foreknowledge, holds that even if the future is ontologically open, it is nonetheless epistemologically closed by God's knowledge. That is, even if the future is such that creatures can freely act in ways that God desires or detests, their free acts are not epistemically hidden from God's absolute knowledge. But if hope requires the hoper to be less than certain, then, by this view, God cannot hope for good uses of creaturely freedom.

There are obvious limits to what God can know. God cannot know what is false, given that knowledge necessarily entails what is true. God cannot know what it is to lie or to sin since these go against God's own

---

44. Molinism, most basically, is that God has complete and absolute knowledge of all necessary and possible truths. This includes what all free persons would do in all possible worlds. God chooses which possible world to actualize and, according to supporters, absolutely knows the future including future free human choices.

nature. But is it possible for God to know creaturely future free contingent acts? For Ward, God cannot.

Ward argues that creation subjects God to certain limitations, even if these limitations were freely chosen by God. "Creation is thus in one sense a self-limitation of God." Not only is God's power limited by free agents, "His knowledge is limited by the freedom of creatures to actualize genuinely new states of affairs, unknown to him until they happen."[45] While it is too long to detail here, Ward insists that it is not possible for even an omniscient being to know future free conditionals. Ward's key point is this, "If God knows eternally what I will do in the future, then it seems that my acts must be fully determined in advance; so, I cannot be free, in the sense that, at the moment of action, I can act otherwise than I do."[46]

Here we see that Ward's conception of God meets a third criterion for a theology of divine hope, that God cannot know with full certainty what I will freely do in the future. If God cannot know many of my future actions, then it is possible that God might hope that I act one way even though it seems that I might act another way. But once again, while it is necessary that creaturely freedom be such that even God cannot know future free choices before they are made, this is not sufficient for God having hope. It may be that God is unaffected by our choices, be they good or bad. For hope to be a genuine divine attribute it is necessary that God is in some sense affected by our choices.

Passibility

Is it possible that this creation is but merely an experiment performed by God? That God is the temporal creator who gives creatures real freedom and cannot know what choices they will make but that God is unaffected by those choices? While I know of no theologians who explicitly hold such a view, it is nonetheless possible.

Most theologians who argue that God is unaffected by this world make their case by arguing that God is unable to be affected. Impassibility, the notion that God is incapable "of being acted upon and having one's emotional experience changed by an external force,"[47] has a long theological history. The doctrine is the logical consequence of divine immutability,

---

45. Ward, *Rational Theology and the Creativity of God*, 84.
46. Ward, *Rational Theology and the Creativity of God*, 130.
47. Sirvent, *Embracing Vulnerability*, 38.

the claim that God is incapable of change, which is itself the logical consequence of other supposed divine attributes, such as simplicity, pure actuality, and perfection.

Ward, like many twentieth-century and twenty-first-century theologians, rejects the idea that divine perfection necessitates an unmoved God. "I am not at all convinced it would be a symptom of perfection to lack all feeling. God, of course, has no senses and no nervous system; whatever feelings he might have are unlikely to be very similar to human feelings. But are we to say that he does not appreciate the beauty of creation at all? That he takes no pleasure in well-doing and feels no sorrow at sin?"[48] Part of God's omniscience is to know how we feel. Not as an outside observer, but as one "sharing in the pain and suffering of the universe."[49]

A temporal God who desires particular future states that are partly dependent on unknowable future free human choice combined with the notion that God is affected by that choice can be said to be a God who hopes. To desire future states that are possible but uncertain, even for God, means that God would hope that those states obtain. However, this is but the thinnest sense of hope. I can imagine a God who desires and demands obedience and thus logically hopes we obey. When there is sin or rebellion this God is angered or frustrated by our actions. Or worse, perhaps God is malevolent and only hopes that others feel pain and suffering. Our sufferings might delight God and so God might hope that we do not stumble into happiness. Or perhaps God is not malevolent but is only hoping that we avoid sin or experience joy for God's sake—that is, not because of an intrinsic concern for human happiness but only because God is necessarily affected by our lives. In this sense God would only be hoping for our pleasure as an instrument of God's pleasure. While these are improbable, such possibilities necessitates that I do not stop here.

The scenario so far is, at best, God *hopes that* some future state will obtain or that some desired proposition will become true. A detached God watching from a distance could have the same hopes. The Christian conception is that God is active in the world, reconciling it to Godself. A Christian understanding of God requires a richer theology of divine hope, one grounded in love.

---

48. Ward, *Rational Theology and the Creativity of God*, 132.
49. Ward, *Rational Theology and the Creativity of God*, 198.

Love

I am finishing this discussion of the divine attributes that ground a theology of divine hope by discussing what many theologians would say is the first or greatest attribute of God. In fact, many argue that it is only because "God is love" that God created genuinely autonomous beings whose free actions affect God. But many other theologians argue that God is love while maintaining many or all the classical ideas about God. Ward speaks of divine love grounding human autonomy, writing, "a God of love may generate persons in order to express the divine love. But those persons will have their own relative autonomy and may express their creativity in opposition to the divine will for them."[50] In this section I aim to show that Ward's conception of God as love not only allows for God to hope but also necessitates that God hope for and in created persons who "can help create forms of goodness—forms of excellence won by effort and discipline, cooperation, and compassion—that otherwise would not have existed."[51]

The fullness of divine love is best understood in the triad of motive, means, and ends. God's love for us is what motivates God to work by all means possible, including by way of death itself, to accomplish God's desired end of unifying all things in God. Said another way, God lovingly works towards a loving end out of a desire for love. But, according to Ward, God is unable to accomplish this loving end unilaterally. As we have seen, Ward argues that God's omnipotence is limited by love, but it is only by love that God can accomplish God's desired ends. "The divine perfection is most fully expressed in an interactive, responsive, and creative love, whose purpose is to draw all creatures from self-imposed isolation of their fallen self-regard to a sharing in the communal reality of divine love." God draws free creatures and "seeks to persuade them to love goodness for itself, and to love God for the intrinsic perfection of the divine being."[52]

Too often hope is thought of as passivity, anxious idleness, waiting for the good desired to obtain. However, an additional feature of hope is that it anticipates. That is, one who has hope takes "whatever present steps or actions one can, in order to [help] bring it about that a future good will obtain."[53] Hope means God is not only patient when patience is needed but

---

50. Ward, *The Christian Idea of God*, 136.
51. Ward, *The Christian Idea of God*, 137.
52. Ward, *Religion and Creation*, 239.
53. Sessions, *The Concept of Faith*, 124.

God is also *active*, working to obtain what is hoped for. Loving a free agent means working for and with that agent to bring about their highest good. Hope therefore is active and living, not merely appreciative but effective.

A love of this kind is not determining; so, it must be hopeful. God is working to bring God's ultimate plan to completion, but this plan is not dependent on God alone. "God will seek to heal and annul the power of self-destruction but will not compel finite minds to love the good and renounce evil—which compulsion would in fact be incompatible with any free assent to love. Thus, divine causality is the patient attraction of love, the influence of which may be gentle and persuasive but which in the end is stronger than death."[54] God is hardly powerless, but God's loving power requires God to be patient in the hope that it will be successful in persuading other minds to love the good and unite with God.

While it may feel ignoble to say, I will say it anyway: just as God is our hope, we are God's hope. The universe will not be what God's desires it to be without our cooperation. "We are agents who have a part to play in bringing the physical universe into union with God, in uniting the physical and spiritual in one sacramental unity."[55] In this sense God does not merely hope *that* some desired state obtains, God's hope is greater, riskier, and far more loving than that. God hopes *in* us and not simply *for* us. The divine plan, in some real sense, depends on our cooperation. It is because "God does not compel humans to do what God wants," and so "in a sense God's intentions can be frustrated," that God rightly puts God's hopes in the humans God has created. In this sense, God is trusting God's own handiwork but also trusting and hoping in all human creatures to respond positively to God's calling.

LOOSE ENDS?

I have sought to demonstrate that a theology of divine hope is more than plausible provided that God, in time, cooperates with free beings—whose future choices are unknowable—to bring about a loving unity of the divine and human. Furthermore, I have argued that Ward's theology is suitable for grounding just such a claim. But there are still some loose ends that need attention. I will address these issues in the form of questions.

---

54. Ward, *The Christian Idea of God*, 207.
55. Ward, *The Christian Idea of God*, 211.

Does a theology of divine hope mean that God cannot guarantee a "plan for the fullness of time, to gather up all things in him, things in heaven and things on earth"? (Eph 1:10). As Ward claims, "If it is God's plan to unite everything in heaven and earth in Christ, then this plan is not ultimately frustratable."[56] Can we rightly say that God's plan cannot be frustrated even if it is somewhat dependent on free finite creatures? Ward offers what is sometimes referred to as a low- or limited-risk open theism. It is low risk because God is guaranteed, ultimately, to get what God desires, even if there are some losses. According to Ward, "what is partly frustratable is not necessarily wholly frustratable. It is logically possible that God's will that I always do good is frustrated, and yet God's will that I find fulfillment in God is not frustratable, since I have been created to seek such fulfillment."[57] If it is certain that God ultimately gets what God desires, then isn't hope impossible, or at least unnecessary, for God?

Some have argued that because all persons have libertarian freedom and all can finally reject God's love, there is no low-risk open theism, only high-risk.[58] If this is true, then God will employ hope all the more. But even in low-risk open theism, hope is necessary, even if a collective "win" is guaranteed. God will rightly hope that the possible few who are hellbent on rejecting God's love will eventually relent. Furthermore, even if universal salvation is ultimately guaranteed, God will rightly work in our lives in the hope of helping us avoid or minimize unnecessary pains and sufferings. It should not be assumed that God is only invested in the endgame; God's love for each creature means that God works and hopes for our daily lives.

Hope is most often contrasted with fear or despair. Those who desire a particular state (for example, the recovery of health for a gravely ill loved one) but do not have hope that the desired state will materialize will naturally fear or despair the impending state. Does this mean that when God desires a certain state that God knows is impossible even God will fear and despair? Are fear and despair the only logical responses to an impossible but desired state?

While fear and despair are natural feelings of hopelessness, they are not necessary feelings. Many who lose hope are not overcome with despair. Many find quiet resignation. They accept the impending state but are not overcome or plagued by feelings of fear or despair. It also does seem

---

56. Ward, *Religion and Creation*, 263.
57. Ward, *Religion and Creation*, 263.
58. Grossl and Vicens, "Closing the Door on Limited-Risk Theism," 475–85.

inappropriate to attribute such feelings to God. God can know what fear and despair are like by sharing in our feelings and pains, but this is quite different from God experiencing first-order despair or fear. First, God as a perfect being will know of possibilities we simply cannot conceive. God may know there is hope while we resign ourselves to hopelessness. Furthermore, God is able to do what is seemingly impossible to us. Therefore, there may be far fewer occasions that God must be resigned to complete hopelessness. Even if a desired situation is not possible, God will likely feel something akin to frustration, disappointment, or sadness; but despair seems impossible for a perfect being since despair leads to inaction and passivity in the pursuit of good. God, however, is always working for good.

CONCLUSION

In this essay I have sought to demonstrate that a theology of divine hope is not only possible but is deeply consonant with conceptions of God like Ward's. A temporal God who, because of love, is limited in knowledge and power by the free choices of created persons but nonetheless seeks the cooperation of those persons in the accomplishment of desired ends would seem to need to hope. Ward is not the only theologian to envision God's nature and relationship with a dynamic creation in this way, but Ward's body of work, with its remarkable width and depth, can provide gravitas to a theology of divine hope.

While Ward's theology does not explicitly detail what it means for God to hope, it nonetheless proclaims God's hope.

> Whatever God "intends inevitably" I had it reversed. comes about. But even God cannot intend on behalf of another rational creature; he can hope, "wish or desire". And those hopes not only can be, but are constantly thwarted; that is precisely the import of moral evil and sin. The whole idea of creation as a form of Divine self-giving, a love which goes out of itself to a freely responsive object, entails that God puts himself at the disposal of creatures, and limits himself in relation to them.[59]

God, then, is limited by, and at the disposal of, creatures; and thus, God has hope in these creatures to do what it is God desires.

---

59. Ward, *Rational Theology and the Creativity of God*, 83.

BIBLIOGRAPHY

Brueggemann, Walter. *Genesis. Interpretation: A Bible Commentary for Teaching and Preaching.* Atlanta: John Knox, 1982.

Calvin, John. *Institutes of the Christian Religion.* 2 vols. Edited by John McNeil, translated by Ford Lewis Battles. Library of Christian Classics. Philadelphia: Westminster, 1960.

Cessario, Romanus. "The Theological Virtue of Hope." In *The Ethics of Aquinas,* edited by Stephen Pope, 232–33. Washington, DC: Georgetown University Press, 2002.

Day, J. P. "Hope." *American Philosophical Quarterly* 6.2 (1969) 89–102.

Feinberg, John. "God Ordains All Things." *Predestination & Free Will: Four Views on Divine Sovereignty & Human Freedom,* edited by David Basinger and Randall Basinger, 17–43. Downers Grove, IL: IVP, 1986.

Fretheim, Terrance E. "The Repentance of God: A Key to Evaluating Old Testament God-Talk." *What Kind of God? Collected Essays of Terrance E. Fretheim,* edited by Michael J. Chan and Brent A. Strawn, 40–57. Winona Lake, IN: Eisenbrauns, 2015.

Grossl, Johannes, and Leigh Vicens. "Closing the Door on Limited-Risk Theism." *Faith and Philosophy* 31.4 (2014) 475–85.

Helm, Paul. "Classical Calvinist Doctrine of God." In *Perspective on the Doctrine of God,* edited by Bruce A. Ware, 5–52. Nashville: Broadman & Holman, 2008.

Holtzen, Wm. Curtis. *The God Who Trusts: A Relational Theology of Divine Faith, Hope, and Love.* Downers Grove, IL: IVP Academic, 2019.

Kazor, Christopher. *Thomas Aquinas on Faith, Hope, and Love: Edited and Explained for Everyone.* Naples, FL: Sapientia Press of Ave Maria University, 2008.

Martin, Adrienne M. *Hope We Hope: A Moral Psychology.* Princeton: Princeton University Press, 2014.

Morgan, Teresa. *Roman Faith and Christian Faith: Pistis and Fides in the Early Roman Empire and Early Churches.* Oxford: Oxford University Press, 2015.

Niebuhr, H. Richard. "Reflections on Faith, Hope, and Love." *The Journal of Religious Ethics* 2.1 (1974) 151–56.

Olson, Roger E. "The Classical Free Will Theist Model of God." In *Perspective on the Doctrine of God,* edited by Bruce A. Ware, 148–72. Nashville: Broadman & Holman, 2008.

Reimer. David J. "An Overlooked Term in Old Testament Theology: Perhaps." *Covenant as Context: Essays in Honour of E. W. Nicholson,* edited by A. D. H. Mayes and R. B. Salters, 325–46. New York: Oxford University Press, 2003.

Sessions, William Lad. *The Concept of Faith: A Philosophical Investigation.* Ithaca, NY: Cornell University Press, 1994.

Sirvent, Roberto. *Embracing Vulnerability: Human and Divine.* Eugene, OR: Pickwick, 2014.

Ward, Keith. *The Big Questions in Science and Religion.* West Conshohocken, PA: Templeton Foundation, 2008.

———. *The Christian Idea of God: A Philosophical Foundation for Faith.* Cambridge: Cambridge University Press, 2017.

———. *Concepts of God: Images of the Divine in Five Religious Traditions*. Oxford: Oneworld, 1987.

———. *God: A Guide for the Perplexed*. Oxford: Oneworld, 2002.

———. *God, Chance, and Necessity*. Oxford: Oneworld, 1996.

———. "Is God a Person?" In *By Faith and Reason: The Essential Keith Ward*, edited by Wm. Curtis Holtzen and Roberto Sirvent, 65–73. London: Darton, Longman, and Todd, 2012.

———. *The Living God*. London: SPCK, 1984.

———. *Rational Theology and the Creativity of God*. New York: Pilgrim, 1982.

———. *Religion and Creation*. Oxford: Oxford University Press, 1996.

———. *Sharing in the Divine Nature: A Personalist Metaphysics*. Eugene, OR: Cascade, 2020.

Waterworth, Jayne M. *A Philosophical Analysis of Hope*. New York: Palgrove Macmillan, 2004.

Wittgenstein, Ludwig. *Philosophical Investigations*. New York: Macmillan, 1953.

Keith Ward's Response to Wm. Curtis Holtzen

THIS IS AN EXCELLENT defense of the assertion that it is proper to say that God hopes, as well as has faith and love. As Curtis says, hope is desire for a future good that is possible but not inevitable, may be difficult to achieve, and may motivate action to make that good come about. If this is the case, hope is only possible for a being that faces an undetermined future with a desire for it that may not be fulfilled. This at once threatens many conceptions of God, which claim that God cannot have unfulfilled desires and for whom there are no unknown or undetermined futures.

Some theologians have held that, as the almighty creator of all things other than Godself, God must either determine or at least know everything that will ever happen, and God desires, or wills, everything that exists. As Curtis says, I do not think this is a logical entailment of creation. God could create beings that control much of their own future, rather than creating beings that are completely under the control of the creator. Then God would not know some of what was going to happen until these beings had decided it. God might decide which possibilities were open to those beings, but would not unilaterally decide which possibilities were chosen. If God had in mind what God thought were the best possibilities, God might hope that they would be chosen, and might seek to influence creaturely choices in some way, but could not completely control what actually happened.

Such a God would not be powerless. God could set out the possibilities that could be chosen, and God might arrange possibilities so as to ensure that a specific divine goal could be realized, despite many disappointing choices that could be made on the way to it. God's will could often be frustrated, but God's final goal would be achieved. This is what Curtis calls "limited-risk open theism." It seems logically possible.

Why would God do such a thing? The answer usually given is that there is something of great value in freely given love, which is not forced. This is true, but modern science can help to show that there is more to it. The universe is now seen as evolving from a primal "Big Bang" by millions of gradual steps to form complex integrated communities of conscious organisms. These organisms are able to act in order to realize envisaged values, and thus consciousness, purpose, and value emerge through the process of cosmic evolution.

Evolution occurs through the interplay of two basic forces. One is survival through competition and natural selection. The other is the emergence of consciousness through cooperation and the gradual development of understanding, moral awareness, and intentional action. Both forces are necessary to the evolution of beings that know, feel, and act from the basic physical elements of the universe. But it is easy for them to become unbalanced and in conflict. That is what has happened on this planet. That is what Christian faith aims to correct.

Humans are emergent, developing beings, parts of a cosmic process towards the greater self-understanding and self-direction of the universe itself. They contribute to this process through learning and creative experimentation. Humans are not, as some myths of Adam and Eve have supposed, originally super-intelligent beings who have fallen from grace into ignorance. They are parts of an emergent cosmic process that is moving from unconscious law-governed states towards states of fully conscious and value-directed action.

There is distinctive value in this developing evolutionary process. The partly self-realizing carbon-based creatures that we are can contribute many sorts of creative value to the process. Love—cooperation in seeking truth, beauty, and goodness—is a major goal of this process. But it is the process of evolutionary emergence itself that is of immense value, and the underlying reason for the creation of humans as one sort of self-creating beings whose destiny is, after many disappointments and failures, to achieve conscious union with the supreme Mind of the cosmos.

The idea of God as a cosmic Mind who is capable of love and hope is fully consonant with this picture of cosmic emergence, and I think it helps us to understand in a new way the God who sets before us the final union of all things in Christ as the goal of creation.

DISCUSSION QUESTIONS

1. How does Holtzen address Niebuhr's concern that attributing hope to God is overly anthropomorphic?

2. Summarize Ward's views on divine temporality, omnipotence, omniscience, and passability. How do these views challenge or support traditional theological perspectives?

3. Which theological views give the best grounding for the concept of divine hope?

4. Ward argues that natural selection and competition were necessary for the evolution of thinking, feeling beings that can exercise creative freedom. Do you agree? Why or why not?

5. Must God either determine everything that will happen or at least know everything that will happen? Why or why not?

6. Consider the practical implications of a theology of divine hope for religious believers. How might this understanding of God's hope influence their actions, prayers, and overall faith experience?

4

Keith Ward and a Metaphysics of Love

THOMAS JAY OORD

IN THE FOLLOWING, I conduct a thought experiment. I aim to answer this question: What metaphysical scheme best accounts for divine and creaturely love?

While my own convictions align with a particular form of Christianity, the metaphysics I seek would apply to love in most, if not all, religious traditions. It would apply also to the love expressed by those who do not identify with *any* religion. The most adequate metaphysics would draw from the love we know in our personal relationships, understood in various scientific disciplines, and witnessed to in sacred texts.

The general claim I defend in this chapter can be stated succinctly: Keith Ward's metaphysical scheme accounts for love better than alternatives.

WHAT IS LOVE?

We cannot make much progress identifying a metaphysics that accounts for love if we do not know what love is. Love is given wildly diverse definitions and meanings, however, and the cacophony can confuse. Progress toward identifying an adequate definition of love requires sifting and sorting, gleaning and synthesizing. The work is imprecise. But if love plays the prominent role that many of the wisest people claim it does, this work matters.

The most common understandings of love include words like . . .

- feeling
- action
- values
- freedom
- God
- relations
- experience
- persons
- motives
- well-being
- justice
- flourishing

It's a tall order to draw together this diverse group of words. Each requires a full-length book to explore and explain sufficiently. But love understood in sacred texts, scientific exploration, and everyday experience points to these words and their synonyms. So we cannot ignore them.

To my knowledge, Keith Ward does not offer a precise definition of love. But his metaphysical vision employs these words in many constructive ways. Ward also makes statements about love that align with the words and ideas above. He says, for instance, that "God loves everything, in the sense of caring for its well-being."[1] Love is relational, he says, and even "God creates and relates personally to minds other than its own."[2] Ward claims that love involves "an affective component" and "implies an active element."[3] In these comments and *many* more, Keith Ward uses the lexicon of love.

To save time, I offer a definition of love I think Ward would endorse, at least broadly speaking. Given the lexicon above and various meanings of the words, we might define love by this three-clause sentence:

> Persons love when they act intentionally, in relational response to God and others, to promote overall well-being.

So defined, love involves feeling, action, values, freedom, God, relations, persons, motives, well-being, and more. Loves act with the motive

---

1. Ward, *Morality, Autonomy, and God*, 210.
2. Ward, *Sharing in the Divine Nature*, 23.
3. Ward, *Sharing in the Divine Nature*, 47.

to promote flourishing, and desires, feelings, and relations influence this motive. Love so defined says that God is an actor who plays a necessary role in inspiring love, and in this role, God provides freedom to others without controlling them. Love's aim is overall well-being, which involves acting justly; it does not neglect some while others are unduly privileged. It also includes self-care and enemy love.

I suspect Keith Ward will generally agree with these statements. But he may add elements or phrase things differently. Most importantly, the elements of the definition of love are central concerns in Ward's work and the idealist metaphysics he embraces.

In the rest of this essay, I argue that Keith Ward's thought supports and expands key ideas in this love definition. As I see, both the metaphysics he adopts and the particular version of Christianity he embraces accounts for love better than primary alternatives.

At the conclusion of this chapter, I suggest minor additions to Ward's proposal and seek his responses to them. As I see it, these adjustments further enhance the conceptual coherency of Ward's contributions to a metaphysics of love.

MIND

Keith Ward believes mind is the ontological and methodological starting point for making sense of reality. Mind is the "priority," he says, and "any theory that denies or ignores experiences and thoughts *must* be wrong."[4] This commitment is the heart of idealist metaphysics.

For Ward, of course, it's his own mind that tries to make sense of himself, God, creatures, and creation. But what is true for Ward is true to varying degrees for others: we have minds by which relate to ourselves, others, God, and existence. We deny this reality at the peril of self-contradiction; to deny this means failing to account for the evidence we know best.

It may seem obvious—in fact, common sense—that minds are required to make sense of reality. "Making sense" is a mindful activity, after all. But Ward's idealism and its emphasis upon the priority of mind is uncommon ... at least among many who take contemporary science seriously. Materialism, rather than idealism, is the metaphysical assumption among many philosophers of science.

---

4. Ward, *The Priority of Mind*, 5.

KEITH WARD AND A METAPHYSICS OF LOVE

Keith Ward opposes the reductive form of materialism, which assumes or states we best understand existence as consisted entirely of mindless matter. "There is a major intellectual battle going on," writes Ward, "between those who adopt a purely materialist view of human persons and those who believe that there is a distinctive reality and value about human minds." Idealists like Ward believe "minds far transcend their physical embodiment, both in their nature and in their moral worth." Those who reject the reality of mind as something distinct from matter and who also "have a grand metaphysical theory about what kinds of things exist," he says, "will probably end up some sort of materialist."[5]

Idealism comes in many forms, and Keith Ward prefers some forms over others. Each shares the belief that "mental events are the most real thing we humans know. We know we have sense-experiences, bodily sensations, thoughts, feelings, and images."[6] This does *not* mean, says Ward, that matter is an illusion—at least for the form of idealism he embraces. Matter is also real, and any adequate metaphysics must account for it.[7]

Lovers have or are minds. But mindful lovers change moment by moment, and this changing requires some account for both the dynamism and continuity inherent in loving people. Keith Ward offers both when he says persons have "a unity of experience" and a "unity of succession in consciousness." That is, "one and the same person continues to exist if there is a unitary consciousness of co-present elements that flows smoothly and continuously through time without gaps, in ways that have at least partly been consciously and intentionally envisaged, evaluated, and chosen."[8]

Ward opposes substantival views of the self that require an unchanging core to personhood. "We don't have to say that there is some indivisible and undetectable substance that continues underneath all the changing states and properties," he says, which comprise a person.[9] The future me will have "temporal continuity between successive sets of private experiences . . . 'I' am constituted by a present unique set of experiences and actions, which continues into the future."[10]

---

5. Ward, *More than Matter*, 11.
6. Ward, *More than Matter*, 23.
7. Ward, *Sharing in the Divine Nature*, 20.
8. Ward, *More Than Matter*, 67-68.
9. Ward, *More Than Matter*, 69.
10. Ward, *More Than Matter*, 72.

This concept of personal continuity and change is crucial to account both for the identities of those who love and for the dynamism of love expressions. In an evolutionary world, the successive states of personal experiences provide conceptual reason to praise persons who love and blame those who do not. This dynamism and continuity also account for love as a particular act in a moment and as the development of persons with loving characters who love repeatedly.

This priority of mind is not limited to humans. In fact, Ward believes we best make sense of existence if we speculate that an ultimate Mind undergirds all that exists. "There is a reality underlying our everyday experience whose basic character is consciousness or mind," he says.[11] For Ward, "mind is the ultimate reality" and "the physical world would not exist without mind as it source."[12] I'll address Ward's views on this ultimate Mind in a later segment.

VALUES

We might imagine a metaphysical scheme that says minds exist but values do not. But it's difficult if not impossible to imagine a metaphysics that said values exist but minds do not. "There are no actual values unless someone values them," says Ward. So minds are "necessary for there to be any actual values in the universe."[13] Because values are essential to understanding love, I explore some of Ward's thoughts on values in this segment.

Value is an "irreducible reality, known to us immediately and by acquaintance," says Ward.[14] "We act in order to reach some goal that we value and set for ourselves," he says, "or maybe to avoid something that we think will give us pain."[15] Humans differ from computers, for instance, because humans "can ask what is valuable about their existence and can set themselves to pursue things that they find to be of value."[16]

Keith Ward criticizes metaphysical schemes that do not or cannot account for the values we all experience. This is the heart of his criticism of reductive materialism, which differs from what he calls "a personal,

11. Ward, *More Than Matter*, 20.
12. Ward, *Sharing in the Divine Nature*, 120.
13. Ward, *More Than Matter*, 89.
14. Ward, *The Priority of Mind*, 29.
15. Ward, *The Priority of Mind*, 22.
16. Ward, *The Priority of Mind*, 31.

experience-centered" approach to existence. A purely materialist approach "does not speak of love, of duty, of aesthetic appreciation, or of friendship," he says, "even though these things are the heart and reality of human existence."[17]

The reductive materialist paints a picture of the world without values, purpose, or meaning. This is ironic, says Ward, because "a highly purposive, valuable, and meaningful activity has to be engaged in to produce a theory that nature has no purpose, values, or meaning."[18] If the one who explains reality is trying to help people make sense of things, the explaining materialist who denies values and purpose but tries to help engages in self-contradictory exercise.

Any metaphysics that denies values or has no conceptual space for them cannot explain well our experiences of love, including the morality inherent in love. Morality assumes better and worse, more helpful and less helpful, and so on. Those are value claims.

It makes no sense to say creatures are morally responsible if values are illusory. "Moral views presuppose metaphysical theories of human nature," says Ward. Materialist metaphysics "sit uneasily" with belief in objective moral values.[19] By contrast, a theistic metaphysics of value "provides a metaphysical context that gives moral claims . . . a clear objectivity and authority, and a distinctive form of motivation that is rarely found in non-theistic views."[20]

Reference to values and morality leads naturally to questions of creaturely agency. Keith Ward believes persons have a measure of autonomy and freedom to make real choices in relation to other minds and the material world. "Human creativity and freedom, human purpose and intention," he says, "are fundamental features of human experience and knowledge."[21]

Creaturely agents choose among futures when they act, because they "possess some degree of freedom," says Ward. "There are a number of different possible futures on each occasion of action," he says, because "the

---

17. Ward, *The Priority of Mind*, 28.
18. Ward, *The Priority of Mind*, 33.
19. Ward, *Morality, Autonomy, and God*, 215.
20. Ward, *Morality, Autonomy, and God*, 212.
21. Ward, *Priority of Mind*, 15.

future is to some extent open."[22] But free agents are not isolated; they "exist as persons in a community of persons."[23] All freedom rests in relations.[24]

The foregoing illustrates that the idealist metaphysics and its emphasis upon values and creaturely freedom supports central features in a coherent view of love. After all, love, as typically understood, involves intentions and values. It is also relational; lovers are not isolated units uninfluenced by others. In fact, we always express the freedom of love in such relations. The options of love are constrained to the context and possibilities pertaining thereto.

To put this negatively, love makes no sense in reductive materialist metaphysics. Such materialist schemes assume that values, freedom, and subjective experience are epiphenomenal. Matter cannot think, feel, or intentionally relate, after all. By contrast, love—creaturely and divine—requires these capacities. And the idealist metaphysics Ward endorses provides a conceptual framework to account for these essential elements of love.

GOD

Keith Ward believes an adequate account of love requires an equally adequate account of God. He believes God is the chief exemplar of love and the ultimate Mind making creaturely love possible.

For Ward, a Christian description of God is "guided by the key teaching that 'God is love.'"[25] But just about every Christian believes God loves. The way many professional theologians conceive of God, however, does not align with love as I have defined it, as we experience it, or as described in much of sacred Scripture. Keith Ward's concept of God is different; it aligns with love so understood.

Unlike the voluntarist God of some theologies, Ward believes God *must* love. God cannot freely choose evil.[26] In fact, divine freedom is "necessarily conditioned" by love.[27] To put this in my own terms, he believes love comes logically prior in the divine nature to will.

22. Ward, *Priority of Mind*, 16.
23. Ward, *Priority of Mind*, 23.
24. Ward, *Priority of Mind*, 16.
25. Keith Ward, *Christ and Cosmos*, 86.
26. Keith Ward, *Christ and Cosmos*, 167.
27. Keith Ward, *Christ and Cosmos*, 165.

We should reject theologies aligned with ancient Greek philosophical notions of a static God, says Ward. Such theologies consider God a timeless substance rather than a dynamic person. They present God as simple, immutable, and impassible too, which fails to align with the dominate biblical portrayal of God or with the personal piety of believers.[28]

Keith Ward agrees with the majority portrayal of God in the Christian Scripture, which portrays God as "a dynamic, creative, and relational reality."[29] This dynamic God changes and is not in all ways immutable. "A general biblical account of God," says Keith, "is more sympathetic to the view that God changes in some respects than to the view that God is completely changeless."[30] A changing God "capable of new creative actions is more supreme than a being that cannot be other than it is."[31]

Keith Ward is what I call an "open and relational theologian," because he believes God essentially experiences time analogous to the way creatures experience it. God's experience is temporal, but the divine nature does not change. Ward rejects the classic view of divine simplicity, because it undermines the personal and relational aspects of God. God does not have a preordained plan that is worked out in a predetermined and precise way.[32]

A relational God suffers with and knows creatures experientially. God's "concern for the well-being of creatures implies knowledge of their condition," says Ward. And it implies "pity if it involves suffering, revulsion if it involves the willful causing of suffering, and action to relieve that suffering where it is possible." A God who simply contemplates suffering "is not truly love." "The one who truly loves will do something to help."[33] God is passible, because "affected by the beauties and sufferings of the created world."[34]

Love compelled God to create the universe. "One who believes in the existence of God," argues Keith Ward, "will believe that there is an actual case of supreme goodness that has created the world for the sake of good."[35] And God had a particular aim in creating: "that autonomous persons can

---

28. Keith expresses this throughout his book *Sharing in the Divine Nature*.
29. Ward, *Christ and Cosmos*, 72.
30. Ward, *Christ and Cosmos*, 61.
31. Ward, *Christ and Cosmos*, 73.
32. Ward, *Sharing in the Divine Nature*, 77–78.
33. Ward, *Sharing in the Divine Nature*, 47.
34. Ward, *Sharing in the Divine Nature*, 49.
35. Ward, *Morality, Autonomy, and God*, 208.

come into existence." These creaturely persons would be able to "shape their own lives freely and creatively, and can find their fulfillment in being united to the divine in love."[36]

In a certain sense, says Ward, God needs creation. "If God's love is agape love, love of the other and the imperfect, then that love could not exist without a creation containing possibly imperfect creatures." This does not mean that the universe created God, however. "Creation in no way brings God into being," Keith says, "and it depends wholly upon God in order to exist."[37]

A good number of Christian theologians affirm divine love as necessary among members of the so-called "social Trinity." But Ward thinks "the idea of God as a sort of society is a bad idea."[38] Christians should not think God is comprised of three persons, each with distinct centers of consciousness, distinct freedoms, distinct responsibilities, distinct wills, and distinct relations between one another. This formulation of the Trinity is, he believes, more tritheistic than monotheistic. Rather, God is one; God has one mind and will.

The loving Creator experientially loves and relates with the created world.[39] God's love is *ad extra*. "If God is a relational being characterized by love," Ward reasons, "that relation must be to non-divine persons, and not a sort of secret self-love."[40] We can talk about divine love as in some sense "trinitarian," Ward says, if we identify a "threefold form of divine love—as creating finite persons, relating in love to them, and uniting them to the divine life." This activity "is the manifestation of the supreme goodness of God as creative, self-giving, and universally inclusive love."[41] "If God is agape love," says Keith, "this is love of what is truly other than God, not just love of the divine beauty and self."[42]

God's "plan" for creation is not a detailed blueprint of all that will occur. God does not entirely determine or even foreknow the what the future of the universe will be. But "God wills that creatures cooperate in the work to create new expressions of love and goodness," he says, "and that plan

36. Ward, *Christ and Cosmos*, 231.
37. Ward, *Sharing in the Divine Nature*, 74.
38. Ward, *Christ and Cosmos*, x.
39. Ward, *Christ and Cosmos*, 72.
40. Ward, *Christ and Cosmos*, 182.
41. Ward, *Christ and Cosmos*, 62.
42. Ward, *Sharing in the Divine Nature*, 77.

can take many forms."⁴³ The love plan God entertains is neither unilaterally determining nor willy nilly.

Creaturely love is derived from divine love. We "must learn to love," says Ward, "by learning to share in the divine love."⁴⁴ This learning provides creaturely persons with their purpose. "The highest business of life is to live well in a just and compassionate society," he says, "and to see that living well consists in seeking the true, the good, and beautiful for its own sake." It involves "realizing as fully as possible our positive human potentialities, and then working for a society and a world in which that is a real possibility for all without exception."⁴⁵

Loving creatures hope to experience even greater love after death. "For those who believe themselves to experience something of a God of love," says Ward, "the hope of paradise is the hope of closer knowledge and love of God."⁴⁶ But this closer knowledge and love does not come through divine fiat. God wills that persons "attain their end by their own efforts, in cooperation with the divine . . . ." And "if finite persons are to love and realize themselves in God, there must be more to finite consciousness than the often painful and always inadequate sense of union with the divine that is apparent in ordinary lives."⁴⁷ This "more" is what many theists call "heaven." Even "the hope of heaven," he says, "is entailed by belief in a God of love."⁴⁸

Keith Ward's theistic metaphysics provides a far more adequate account of love, creaturely and divine, than alternatives. Rather than a materialist metaphysics that denies essential elements of love, such as value, freedom, experience, agency, morality, and more, Ward's idealistic metaphysics not only accounts for these elements but emphasizes them. Rather than a theistic metaphysics that claims God is impassible, timeless, simple, and in all ways immutable, Ward's theistic metaphysics portrays dynamic love as the activity of a dynamic God in giving-and-receiving relations with creatures.

Keith Ward's philosophical vision aligns with a robust account of love.

---

43. Ward, *Sharing in the Divine Nature*, 77–78.
44. Ward, *Morality, Autonomy, and God*, 202.
45. Ward, *Morality, Autonomy, and God*, 202.
46. Ward, *Morality, Autonomy, and God*, 207.
47. Ward, *Morality, Autonomy, and God*, 192.
48. Ward, *Morality, Autonomy, and God*, 207.

MINOR ADDITIONS

I conclude with two issues related to love about which, as far as I can tell, Ward and I think differently. The two issues emerge from this question: Can pure Mind create mindless matter?

Ward believes a Mind exists we call "God." This Mind predates the matter that comprises our universe (and any other universe). As far as I can discern from Ward's writings, the Mind he believes predates the matter that makes up this universe has no essential material dimension. I'm calling this "pure Mind."

In some writings, Ward embraces the idea this pure Mind created a wholly material universe, out of which eventually emerged creatures with mental dimensions. This view aligns with a "strong emergence" perspective, whereby entities with mental capacities emerge in an evolutionary process from matter without mentality. Presumably, the pure Mind played a role in this evolutionary emergence.

I have difficulty conceiving how a purely mental Mind can create purely material others. This pure Mind presumably has no hands, feet, claws, or appendages by which to manipulate matter externally. There are no divine fingernails to flick specs of dirt or a divine womb from which purely material quarks literally germinate. Presumably, this pure Mind creates via conceptual or mental influence rather than physical manipulation. But how can purely material entities be influenced by pure mentality?

I think Keith Ward's idealist metaphysics would be more robust if he adopted two ideas. These are ideas he's considered, at least in part. But I want to make a case for their conceptual winsomeness. The first idea: "Reject believing God is pure Mind and any creature can be purely material."

Ward explores what he calls "pluralistic idealism" and "dual-aspect idealism." In one book, he even says, "the form of idealism I am defending . . . could be called dual-aspect idealism."[49] I prefer to call this view "mental-material monism," but I think the two labels can point to similar if identical notions. I propose that mental-material monism not only applies to all creaturely entities, but also to the universal Mind.

Ward is aware of this possibility. He talks appreciatively of "Whitehead's view of the world as a succession of transitory events, each of which has an 'inner' aspect as well as an outward physical appearance." Keith Ward talks about "primitive sentience" as a "function of complex organic

---

49. Ward, *More than Matter*, 92.

forms."⁵⁰ He can embrace dual-aspect idealism so long as 1) "the most important feature of human person is that they are streams or chains of mental acts and events" and 2) "these streams of consciousness are the inner aspects of complex organized physical systems."⁵¹

I affirm the essential features Ward notes. But I would like to add another essential feature. And perhaps the "monism" of my label "mental-material monism" designates the move I want to make that Ward may not. I think it helpful to claim that every being who exists—from quarks to amoeba to worms to cats to humans to angels (if they exist) to even God—are beings with both mental and material aspects.

The mental-material monism I propose can accept Keith's ontological and methodological priority of mind. But mental-material monism assumes beings cannot be *only* minds or *only* material. The degree or complexity of mentality and materiality may differ radically, depending on the entities involved. The rock can be composed of entities with miniscule mentality and organized as an inanimate aggregate. And yet both mentality and materiality obtain. At the other extreme, God's being may be largely composed of mentality and have a level of materiality imperceptible to our five senses. And yet this universal Person also has material and mental dimensions.

To say the divine Mind (who has an aspect of materiality) creates material creatures (who have varying degrees of mentality) goes a long way in explaining how God creates. The divine creator comprised of mentality and materiality creates in relation to creaturely entities whose mentality and materiality differ in degree rather than absolute kind. And because the divine Person is a universal Spirit without a localized body with hands, fingernails, womb, and more, this Person creates primarily, if not exclusively, through mental persuasion. This deity calls for existence, and creation responds.

That God's creating involves creation responding to God leads to the second issue I want to raise. It's another issue Keith Ward has explored, so I hope to represent him accurately. "Reject believing in creation from nothing and affirm instead that God has, in love, everlastingly been creating out of or in relation to what God previously created."

I admire Keith Ward's boldness in making claims about God. He does this humbly, not certain his claims are correct. But he does not shirk from proposing a metaphysics of God and creation he thinks may tell us

---

50. Ward, *More than Matter*, 102.
51. Ward, *More than Matter*, 103.

something true. His claims derive from God's apparent actions in relation to creation. As I see it, a metaphysics of love should build from these divine actions to make claims about God as essentially loving and everlastingly creative. God must love and create.

Ward offers reasons he might accept the creation theory I am suggesting. For instance, he ties divine love with God's creating non-divine others. "Any argument for real love in God would necessitate the creation of truly other, and qualitatively different, persons," he says. "An *agape* loving God would have to create some other persons, but they would be qualitatively different from God and would be chosen from among many alternatives." But he adds that "it is not clear that God necessarily has to love in an agapistic way, even though it might be natural for God to do so."[52]

Some may worry that a metaphysics of love that says God *must* love and *must* create creaturely others binds God into a metaphysical trap, eliminating divine freedom. Ward fends off this criticism. "Logically speaking," he says, "the necessary creation of some universe of finite persons would not impugn the divine freedom, and it would leave the creation of this specific universe and the persons in it as a truly free divine act."[53]

He also wards off the criticism that a God who necessarily loves and creates would overly depend upon creation. "Suppose that God is essentially loving," he says, "then it might be true that this entails that God creates some other object to love.... It does not follow ... that this makes God dependent on creation. It is God alone who wills that creation should exist as a condition of realizing the divine nature as love. That is not a question of God depending on something completely independent of God."[54]

Despite affirming the plausibility of the theory that says God everlastingly creates and loves creatures, Keith Ward is reluctant to embrace it. "If God is essentially love," he says, "then some form of creation of others may indeed be a natural expression of the divine being." But he adds, "that does not mean that God must necessarily and always have created others to love. It means only that the expression of God's nature makes it natural that God will (not necessarily without beginning or intermission or end!) at some point create other persons in order to realize the divine nature as loving in relation to them."[55]

---

52. Ward, *Christ and Cosmos*, 192.
53. Ward, *Christ and Cosmos*, 182.
54. Ward, *Christ and Cosmos*, 194.
55. Ward, *Christ and Cosmos*, 180.

Ward loses me when he makes claims like this: "God does not always have to be creating in order to essentially be a creator."[56] What does it mean to say a property is essential to something, I ask, if that something may or may express that property? Would it make sense to say, for instance, "God does not always have to exist in order for God to exist necessarily"?

"Even supposing that such love entails that God must create an object for God to love," argues Ward, "it seems obvious that this object must be genuinely other than God and need not exist everlastingly but only for a finite time."[57] I agree with him here. I don't think it makes sense to say the creaturely entities God creates exist everlastingly. But if God is to love creaturely others everlastingly, there must everlastingly be creatures whom God loves.

Keith Ward's argument seems best expressed in this paragraph:

> I am not convinced that God can only realize the divine nature by creating a new universe so that creation becomes necessary to God be what God is. But I do accept that God has actually expressed the divine being as agapistic love by the creation of finite persons. I think this must be seen as a normal and proper expression of the divine nature, but I regarded as a step too far to say that this is what God had to do it and that there is no other way in which God could fully be God. Yet even if some creation was necessary to God, that would not make God dependent upon something other than God. God would still be the creator of everything other than God, and creation would then be an essential divine property, rather than, as I think it is, a contingent and gratuitous act of divine grace.[58]

Despite this, he admits that "it might be possible to hold that God, if and in so far as God is truly love, must be related to some form of other being. If so, God necessarily creates something other to which to be related. . . . That is an interesting possibility, though most Christian theologians have not accepted it. I admit that I am half-inclined to accept it, though I draw back at the thought of presuming to know what is necessary for God to be God."[59]

---

56. Ward, *Christ and Cosmos*, 194.
57. Ward, *Christ and Cosmos*, 194.
58. Ward, *Christ and Cosmos*, 220–21.
59. Ward, *Christ and Cosmos*, 124.

I want to urge Ward to move from "half-inclined" to be fully inclined. I think his personal idealism would be more coherent overall and witness more robustly to love if he said God necessarily creates and loves creaturely others everlastingly.

What metaphysical moves might shift Keith Ward from being half inclined to being fully inclined? I suggest a series of claims that build from his own affirmations of God's necessary and contingent aspects.

Ward might say that everlastingly creating and loving creatures is a necessary aspect of God. Creating and loving are essential attributes of the divine nature. This implies that there are always creaturely others whom God has created and whom God loves. In this sense, a realm of creaturely others will always be present, because God creates them.

But Ward might also say the particular creatures God creates and loves are contingent. No single entity, creature, or universe exists necessarily. And because God necessarily exists (*a se*), God does not depend for upon creatures for God's own existence.

In this scenario, God can "fully be God," to use Ward's phrase, and yet also always love and create creaturely others. No entity, creature, or universe would be "an essential divine property," as he puts it. But creating and loving creatures *would* be essential divine properties. The particular creatures God creates in relation to what God created previously would result from a "contingent and gratuitous act of divine grace," to use his language again. But the fact that God graciously creates would be an essential divine property.

Keith Ward moves even closer to this idea in *Sharing in the Divine Nature*. He affirms that "God is necessary in some respects (necessary in existence and in the divine nature as wise and loving), but contingent in others (in divine knowledge of freely chosen creaturely actions)."[60] Then in a response to David Bentley Hart's work, Keith says, "The necessity of creation . . . does not arise from a lack in God, but from the fact that God's love by nature overflows to create persons drawn out of nothing who can come to share in God's love and joy. This love for creation is as necessary to the nature of a God who is love and is not just limited to the divine being itself, as it is the love for other divine persons which, for David Bentley Hart, is part of the necessary nature of God."[61]

---

60. Ward, *Christ and Cosmos*, 61.
61. Ward, *Sharing the Divine Nature*, 74.

I suggest Keith Ward reject saying God creates from nothing but says instead that God necessarily creates new creatures out of or in relation to creatures God previously created. In this, no single creaturely entity or universe is necessary. But it is necessary that *some* creatures exist. This necessity isn't derived from something essential in creatureliness. It's derived from God's nature as Creator.

A HORSE ANALOGY

Admittedly, this metaphysical conversation operates in the realm of abstract speculation, although it has concrete consequences. To illustrate the proposal I'm making, I offer a horse analogy. I mean for it to illustrate, albeit imperfectly, my central proposal to Keith Ward. I propose Ward says that a Mind with mental and material dimensions, in love, everlastingly creates out of or in relation to creaturely others with mental and material dimensions, creaturely others God previously created.

I spend time with and photograph wild horses in Idaho. Sometimes, a stallion can sire generations in a single herd. He impregnates mares, the fillies of those mares, the fillies of those fillies, and so on.

Imagine a stallion who lived a million years. Suppose it's this stallion's nature to bear offspring, and he always relates to at least one mare, but often to many mares during their lifetimes. Suppose the lifespan of a typical mare is twenty-five years.

The stallion in this analogy goes through a succession of sexual relationships with mares who bear offspring. Those offspring bear more offspring. And so on. But no single mare lives a million years alongside the stallion.

We can apply this to the theory of divine creating. I'm saying an everlasting God who by nature always creates and loves creatures will always have others with whom to create and love. But no creaturely other—whether a single entity or universe—is itself everlasting. Each comes and goes. God necessarily creates out of what God previously created and yet no single universe exists necessarily. Because God always creates in relation to what God previously created, there will always be creaturely others.

My alternative creation theory denies that any creaturely materials predate God. God always creates in each moment out of that which God created in the previous. God doesn't create out of "stuff" God never encountered before and never "stumbles upon" something God did not create.

The stallion analogy helps us understand this too, but we'll have to expand it. We speculated this stallion lives a million years and, by nature, relates with and procreates alongside mares. These mares came from his previous procreation with their mothers. The stallion co-creates in relation to what he previously created. In our analogy, he does not "stumble upon" or "find" a mare he had not previously co-created.

Our hypothetical stallion came into existence, of course. He comes from a mare. And he will eventually die. In God's case, procreating in relation with creation had no beginning and will have no end. God exists, loves, and creates everlastingly. But just as the stallion relies upon co-creating mares, God relies upon the contributions of creaturely others.

To say God everlastingly creates and loves in relation to creation means God *needs* creatures. But this Creator "needs" creation in some respects and not others. To say God, in love, always creates out of that which God previously created does not imply God's existence depends upon creatures. God exists necessarily, and nothing can end that.

Although God exists necessarily, God needs creatures because relational love is never solitary. God depends on others with whom God lovingly gives and receives. Because "the steadfast love of the Lord endures forever," God needs creatures to love. As the quotations above show, Keith Ward agrees with this form of divine need.

I add that God also needs creatures in the creative process. This dependence is not about *whether* God creates. God *necessarily* creates, and God's motive to create comes from love. But the *results* of God's creating depend upon creaturely forces, factors, and choices. God's co-creating depends upon the existence of created co-creators.

There is no logical contradiction in saying that, to exist, God does not need creation, *and yet* God needs creation in each moment. So long as there are always creaturely others whom God creates and loves, God can both necessarily exist and necessarily create through dependent relations. In fact, the notion that God necessarily creates *guarantees* God will always have others to love and with whom to co-create.[62]

CONCLUSION

My primary work has been to argue that Keith Ward's metaphysical vision makes better sense of love—creaturely and divine—than alternative

---

62. Find this illustration and other arguments in Oord, *Pluriform Love*.

metaphysics. His idealism overcomes major problems in reductive materialist metaphysics and theistic metaphysics common in what many today call "classical theism." I commend Keith Ward's life work as exceedingly fruitful for making sense of love.

I've also suggested two minor additions to Ward's vision. I've suggested he embrace material-mental monism as applied both to all creaturely entities—simple and complex, aggregate or organismic—and to God. And I've suggested he reject the "creation from nothing" view and embrace the idea that God has everlastingly, in love, created out of or in relation to creaturely others God previously created. As I see this, these minor additions strengthen Keith Ward's already strong love proposals.

BIBLIOGRAPHY

Oord, Thomas Jay. *Pluriform Love: An Open and Relational Theology of Well-Being.* Grasmere, ID: SacraSage, 2022.

Ward, Keith. *Morality, Autonomy, and God.* London: OneWorld, 2013.

———. *More Than Matter: Is There More to Life Than Molecules?* Grand Rapids: Eerdmans, 2010.

———. *The Priority of Mind.* Eugene, OR: Cascade, 2021.

———. *Sharing in the Divine Nature: A Personalist Metaphysics.* Eugene, OR: Cascade, 2020.

Keith Ward's Response to Thomas Jay Oord

I MUST THANK TOM OORD for giving such a positive and accurate account of personal idealism, as I understand it. I heartily agree with just about everything he says. Except for the two modifications that he suggests to my account. Even then, the difference between us is not that we disagree strongly, but that I remain much more agnostic about them than he is.

First, he urges me to adopt a strong mind-matter monism, for which all entities, including God, have both a mental and a physical aspect, which cannot exist apart. I have real problems about God's physical aspect. God certainly has a mental aspect—God knows, thinks, and feels. Yet God has no brain (there is no observable divine brain in the cosmos), so God's thoughts are presumably not located in space, and do not depend upon a physically locatable brain. In that case, God could be a pure Mind. God could have purely intellectual knowledge, and could, in an analogical way, think and imagine and create without forming any physical cosmos. I suspect there could well be a purely mental supreme reality, but I do not know, and I do not see how any human could be sure.

Perhaps the whole physical cosmos could be the body of God (as in Ramanuja). Yet while that is a metaphor that appeals to me, since it locates the cosmos "in" God, it is a *metaphor*, since the cosmos does not have the integrated structure of an organic body.

Oord thinks that creation would be more intelligible if the material cosmos arose from a material basis, because we cannot understand how the purely mental could give rise to the physical. However, I think we cannot understand how anything can give rise to anything else. How could the physical give rise to the mental? Or how could the physical give rise to the physical? Causality is a fundamental mystery to us, and Mind giving rise to matter is no more mysterious than material causality. In fact, as Berkeley said, we are better acquainted with mental causation (in intentional action) then we are with physical. So I do not find the idea of Mind causing matter more than ordinarily mysterious.

The second modification Tom Oord suggests is that, if God is essentially a creator, then there must always be a creation (as Descartes said, if I think therefore I am, then I must be always thinking). The doctrine of creation out of nothing, Tom says, must be false. But this does not seem right. Humans, for instance, are intelligent even when asleep; they do not have to be doing intelligent things all the time. So being essentially a creator does not entail always creating, any more than being essentially rational entails always doing sums.

In fact, if God ever does anything new, that is a form of "creation out of nothing" in the sense that there was nothing of that exact sort in existence before God did that. It was not made out of some pre-existent stuff (except an idea in God's mind, and even that, for a genuine creator, could be quite original). I think that genuine creation means that God can do really new things, that have never existed before. It follows that God can very often create out of nothing, and there is no reason why God should not create a material cosmos when there was not one before (if the word "before" even makes sense here).

With regard to Oord's two proposals, therefore, I remain agnostic. I simply do not think we have any way of knowing whether everything, including God, has both a mental and a physical aspect, and we do not know whether God is always creating. There are no logically compelling arguments in this area. But we can believe, for good reasons, that consciousness and physicality are conjoined in a much larger number of cases than we thought, and that God is essentially creative, though not necessarily in a physical sense. There can, as far as we can see, be purely mental forms of causality.

I think both of Tom Oord's proposals are sensible and theoretically interesting, and I am sometimes half-inclined to them. However, I believe we can have all the advantages they are meant to bring without actually committing ourselves to them.

Keith Ward's Response to Thomas Jay Oord

DISCUSSION QUESTIONS

1. What is love? Do you agree with the account offered by Oord?
2. Do you agree that "Keith Ward's metaphysical vision makes better sense of love—creaturely and divine—than alternative metaphysics"? How would an advocate for a more classical theology respond to this claim?
3. Is the "stallion analogy" helpful in explaining how God creates out of pre-existing material? What are the objections to this analogy?
4. Would you agree that Keith Ward is properly described as a an "open and relational theologian"?
5. Discuss the arguments for and against the material basis for the mental. Is Ward right to find a strong mind-matter monism problematic?
6. How important is the doctrine that God creates out of nothing? To what extent do your agree with Oord's advocacy that the doctrine is unhelpful and Ward's tentative agnosticism?

5

Keith Ward and Pedagogy

J'ANNINE JOBLING

As far as I am aware, Keith Ward has not written explicitly on pedagogy. Nevertheless, I am going to argue here that his work has relevance for and resonance with pedagogical models, including those in non-Christian contexts. Contemporary pedagogy in the Western contexts with which I am familiar has largely moved away from methods reminiscent of Dickens's Gradgrind. Uncertainty, complexity, and the role of social construction in knowledge creation are typically acknowledged.[1] Students are encouraged to engage from a position of agency and critical reflection as active participants. This sits in some tension with increasingly marketized and instrumentalist educational systems. I suggest here that Ward's metaphysical account of Christianity, based in personal idealism, supports and reinforces the impetus to educational models that resist the instrumental. The discussion moves across the following segments: faith, reason, and diversity; process philosophy and cosmology; love; and creativity.

FAITH, REASON, AND DIVERSITY

Within theological circles, the relationship between faith and reason is a long-standing debate. What, asked Tertullian, has Athens to do with Jerusalem? Ward's work offers an admirable example of how faith and reason can stand in mutually enriching constructive theology and philosophy. My interest here is in the process by which this reconciliation is achieved and

1. Watkins and Mortimer, "Pedagogy: What Do We Know?," 2.

the potential significance of this to pedagogy. But first I will expand somewhat on Ward's account of how faith and reason stand together.

Ward's capacity to combine commitment to Christian orthodoxy with commitment to careful, rational, and comparative reflection is one of his methodological hallmarks. He argues that it is possible "to make a firm commitment to Christian revelation while defending to the full the free use of philosophical and critical reasoning."[2] Indeed, this is not only possible, but proper; if the world is created by God through the *Logos*, it is both rational and subject to rational understanding. But such rational understanding is not static. As he says, in theological thinking "there is an essential element of contextualization, as new knowledge from other areas—in the sciences, in philosophy, or in social and political relationships—changes the relationship of religion to those areas."[3] Thus, knowledge is open-ended and subject to the demands of new information. Beliefs change with exposure to knowledge, ways of thinking and perspectives that are new, or at least new to us.

This dynamism extends not only to truths, ideas, and theories emerging from the practice of scientific or philosophical investigation. Potgieter argues that Ward's model of revelation and divine–world relations amounts to a "soft panentheism," which enables continuing experiences of God to include new disclosures of God's love; the love of God then becomes "a basis for Ward's hermeneutic, which allows the church to engage in love as dynamic experience."[4] This, then undergirds a theology that, whilst rooted in faith, is also open to reconceptualization and reimagination. So, Potgieter comments, it is "no surprise to find a quote such as: 'The Bible is a signpost to new exploration of the mind of God, not a barrier to all original thought.'"[5]

As well as being subject to change and development, our knowledge and beliefs are also partial and acculturated; Ward argues that we should not "pretend that our own beliefs are just obviously true and ought to be obvious to all rational people."[6] To Ward, theological thinking is holistic and needs to pay attention to the full panoply of human experience and

---

2. Sirvent and Holtzen, *By Faith and Reason*, 19.

3. Ward, *Religion and Revelation*, 34.

4. Potgieter, "Keith Ward's Soft Panentheism," 5.

5. Potgieter, "Keith Ward's Soft Panentheism," 5. The quote is from Ward, *What the Bible Really Teaches*, 16.

6. Sirvent and Holtzen, *By Faith and Reason*, 22.

human knowledge. This requires a certain global perspective. More, it requires a willingness to participate in this globally conceived community, perceiving theology as "a global discipline, aiming at understanding the truth as a whole."[7]

Pedagogically speaking, I identify two valuable insights here. The first may be classified under the heading "faith and commitment." The second relates to diversity. I shall discuss faith and commitment first.

The primary point to make here is that the understanding of "faith" may be extended beyond adherence to a specific religious tradition. Human beings are not neutral automata, and our broader navigation of the world beyond religious fora is both underpinned and conditioned by social attachments, contexts, and commitments. Michael Sandel develops this argument in critiquing both Rawls and Nozick as espousing forms of deontological liberalism that put the "right" before the "good." This, he claims, involves a false metaphysical view of the person in which the "self" is conceived of as prior to its attachments.[8] For Sandel, far from being "unencumbered" selves, attachments and ends are constitutive of the person. He identifies three particular concerns here:

1. People are related to their own ends voluntaristically, as if from a menu of indefinite possibilities, rather than through cognitive praxis through a process of critical and reflexive self-discovery of self and social world.

2. If a self is constituted "antecedently to its ends," then those ends can never be constitutive of the self. This inserts a gap between the self and what it values as if our ends and what we value are detachable.[9] This, suggests Sandel, does not match our own phenomenological experience. The way in which we may feel profoundly conflicted by competing values and ends supports this.

---

7. Bartel, *Comparative Theology: Essays for Keith Ward*, xii.
8. Sandel, "The Procedural Republic and the Unencumbered Self."
9. Sandel relates this to Rawls' account of the original position, in which one imagines one is making decisions behind a "veil of ignorance." He claims this prioritizes morally the individual autonomy of the choosing subject over the chosen ends. I am not sure this critique of Rawls is entirely fair; the original position is set up as a pragmatic thought experiment to encourage thinking justly and in an other-regarding manner rather than purely on self-interest; it is not a metaphysical construct. As a thought experiment, the limitations are already clear. We do not *really* occupy that detached space behind the veil of ignorance. Rawls himself responded that the "self" of the original position was a political conception of person *qua* citizen, not a posited "true essence."

3. The "unencumbered self" offers an impoverished account of our communal political being. Selves are already encumbered with attachments—such as to family, social groups, nation—which bring with them prior ends, values, and obligations.[10]

This account of the self as socially and politically constituted but not determined seems to me in certain respects analogous to a view of the self as constituted by religious commitment but prepared to engage in rational reflection upon the nature, metaphysics, and implications of this.

This is pedagogically relevant because, if we accept Sandel's account of the self, *all* inhabitants of a classroom are constituted by attachments, commitments, values, and ends. This is not confined to those ostensibly espousing a faith position. The contention here, then, is that the relationship between faith and reason has analogical relevance to other forms of commitments, ends, and values that a person may hold, and it undercuts ideas of learners as passive receptacles or neutral slates, or of knowledge as unproblematically universal.

The second aspect arising I identified for discussion was diversity. Ward, as an exponent of comparative theology, is deeply involved in interfaith analysis. As just argued, faith is in some respects analogous to other positions that a person may hold. And some of those attachments, commitments, values, and ends may well include disagreement and conflict—within the self, within the student body, and between student and teacher.

For example, a teaching assistant colleague, "Jake," was recently taken aback while teaching Plato by a mature male student's insistence that women were less intellectually able than men. Other students, women and men, were incensed. This is a secular example of how people's beliefs actually matter to them, are not only of theoretical concern, and how people's identities may be impacted in classroom contexts. (Potentially, it also highlights how selves can be "encumbered" by dynamics of power and relationality; would the same view have been openly expressed if a senior female academic had been taking the class?)

Ward is speaking with specific reference to religion when he says that "diversity is not a problem," but "natural and good," and that truth is sought through "a process of dialectical interaction."[11] One might extend these sentiments to diversity in thought and beliefs which are not religiously

---

10. Sandel, "The Procedural Republic and the Unencumbered Self."
11. Ward, *Religion in the Modern World*, 7.

rooted. Furthermore, Ward argues that people misunderstand the role of reason in human life. This is self-evident in the scholarly and philosophical disagreements discernible across the entire history of ideas. Reasoning, says Ward, actually results in disagreement:

> Different starting points or axioms seem reasonable to different people, and reasons that seem strong to some people seem weak to others. There is no such thing as completely impartial and universal reason.[12]

Nevertheless, Ward maintains that beliefs can be based on reason, or be held unreasonably. Criteria thus need developing to establish which is which (itself an act of reasoning). Ward identifies clarity of starting point, awareness of implications, avoidance of inconsistencies and confusions, the careful and sympathetic consideration of alternative views, and a readiness to respond to criticism.[13] He also maintains that appeal to authority is not incompatible with the exercise of reason, as long as this does not equate to unquestioning and uncritical acceptance.[14] One must, perforce, be able to justify one's dependence on authority. Climate change, the pandemic, flat earth, QAnon: recent high-profile public controversy on matters related to these illustrate the importance of choosing your experts wisely. Yet even so, there are issues over which even highly credible and well-informed experts can nevertheless disagree. (Ward cites freedom and determinism as an example, with treatment of criminals a possible practical implication.)

So the first consideration is that the self is not unencumbered and, whether a member of a faith community or not, will have their own attachments, commitments, beliefs, values, and ends. The self can subject these to reasoned scrutiny, along with other knowledge and information within their purview. The second consideration is that even when sincerely engaging in this critical act of reflection, disagreements will still arise.

A number of conclusions arise from Ward's reflections on faith and reason that I suggest are validly incorporated into pedagogical models, including within secular contexts.

Firstly, we should be aware of historical particularity. This includes autobiographically, since personal development takes place within contexts—historical, geographical, individual, community. It also includes

---

12. Sirvent and Holtzen, *By Faith and Reason*, 14.
13. Sirvent and Holtzen, *By Faith and Reason*.
14. Sirvent and Holtzen, *By Faith and Reason*.

recognition that beliefs and values themselves have a history—in Nietzschean terms, a genealogy, although acknowledging this does not commit one to Nietzschean conclusions. This leads to a critical and self-reflexive pedagogical model, in which both students and teachers are prepared to interrogate their beliefs and values. This is not necessarily comfortable. It also requires critical interrogation of curriculum choices, as has come to the fore with recent critical attention on colonial history and the history of slavery.

As well, it involves consideration of the beliefs and values of others. Here Ward calls for an approach that aims at sympathetic understanding as well as critical rigor, whilst not exempting one's viewpoints from similar critical interrogation. This means that a pedagogical principle is to extend the scope of scrutiny as far as possible—so that "our knowledge of the world will be both wide and deep, well-informed and fully aware."[15] Yet we also need the humility, whether as teacher or student, to recognize that our knowledge will always fall short of full awareness. This makes it especially important, as a pedagogical value, to pay attention to the thoughts and perspectives of others. It also means we should be especially attentive to the impact of different perspectival knowledge, as called for by various strands of standpoint epistemology.

It is by now widely acknowledged that "difference" in relation to normative positions makes a difference to knowledge, as illustrated by, for example, the histories and lived experience of both women and people of color. This influences not only the character of experience but also the questions posed of the world. For example, phenomenological distinctiveness led to the emergence of black existentialism, or as Gordon put it, "the existential demand for recognizing the situation or lived context of Africana people's being in the world," grounded in philosophical questions concerned with "freedom, anguish, responsibilities, embodied agency, sociality and liberation."[16] It rested on the experience of being black in an anti-black world structured by both racism and racialization as organizing principles. Fanon spoke of the "existential deviation"—that is, the experience of having a language, culture, and identity imposed by the domination of the colonizer,[17] and du Bois talked of "double consciousness"—"this

---

15. Sirvent and Holtzen, *By Faith and Reason*.
16. Gordon, *Existence in Black*, 3–4.
17. Fanon, *Black Skin, White Masks*, 14.

sense of always looking at one's self through the eyes of others."[18] This is not a passing state of mind, but marked by a persistent condition of consciousness caused by a particular socio-political configuration which creates a particular epistemological perspective—such as awareness of the distance between the ideals of democracy and racialized society.

These historical and phenomenological particularities point, pedagogically, to models of learning and teaching that move away from transmission-based models to ones that grant space for student inclusion and active learning. This is not only as a means of fostering student engagement but as a matter of social justice, seeking to incorporate socially just pedagogy by empowering students through partnership in learning, teaching, and assessment processes, and provision of a "space for active participation, autonomy, and power over what will be learned."[19] The tutor's role becomes that of facilitator and, together with the students, creating a dialogic and respectful learning environment of mutual recognition.

The above considerations may also point to what I will call "pedagogical vagueness." I adapt this term from reflections by Polkinghorne and Neville in response to the work of Keith Ward on science, creation, and cosmology in which they discuss "metaphysical vagueness."[20] Neville defines a vague claim as:

> one that does not by itself determine an object but requires further specification, and tolerates specifications that might be contradictory to each other. . . . The vagueness proper to metaphysics should tolerate alternative specifications of its categories by science, but should not tolerate specifications universally thought to be absurd.[21]

If that is the vagueness proper to metaphysics, what is the vagueness I am proposing is proper to pedagogy? I suggest it indicates a model of learning and teaching that is non-determinative, and hosts differences in views and arguments without reductively seeking to flatten student views into a singular "right answer." Of course, there are disciplinary contexts and moments where there may indeed be a "right answer." Yet such is not necessarily

---

18. Du Bois, *The Souls of Black Folk*, 3.

19. Aktas, "Enhancing Social Justice and Socially Just Pedagogy."

20. Polkinghorne, "God, Science and Philosophy" and Neville, "Creation and Cosmology."

21. Neville, "Creation and Cosmology," 129.

yielded even by mathematical problems,[22] and scientists may also disagree over which theories offer the greatest explanatory power. In humanities and social sciences, facts may be well established to greater or lesser degrees, but the interpretation of those facts and the actions proposed in response to them may differ greatly.

The proposal is not, however, to foster an "anything goes" approach. Neville, cited above, excludes specifications thought to be absurd from his metaphysical vagueness; he invokes a criterion of non-arbitrariness, such that resistance to critical inquiry is ruled out, and an openness to critical correction is maintained. This is reminiscent of Ward's criteria.

Pedagogical vagueness relates also to the expected ends. Standardized models of learning include clearly specified learning outcomes, stating what students will know and be able to do by the end of a session or course. This is not in itself a bad thing. Certainly, students complain about vagueness in pedagogy if by this is meant a sense of meandering and lack of any purpose or direction. Clarity of focus is beneficial, and educational systems today are typically led by assessments and award outcomes; teachers have a responsibility to students to ensure they are prepared for these. However, there is the danger that overdetermined approaches to learning teleologies exclude fresh insights, novelty, creativity, and pursuit of awakened interests. For example, sometimes discussions may not head in the anticipated direction, yet it seems to me a diminishment of pedagogy if animated engagement must be cut off to comply with a pre-established concept of what track the students "ought" to have taken. League tables and evaluation frameworks may impose a rigidity of requirement on learning environments that includes the risk of learning and teaching "to the test,"[23] and thus potentially limiting opportunities for students to engage in their own curiosity-led research and development as independent learners and thinkers. (Of course, there are limits to this; one would prefer one's doctor to have acquired certain specific knowledge and skills. On the other hand, there are aspects of the medical profession that do call for development of the capacity to make autonomous, value-based, and interpretative judgments.)

Therefore, I conclude here that Ward's analysis of how faith and reason interrelate has broader potential implications for how differing

---

22. Devlin, "Devlin's Angle: Most Math Problems Do Not Have a Unique Right Answer."

23. See also Kellaghan and Greaney, *Public Examinations Examined*.

commitments and disagreements might be approached in classroom contexts through openness to the other, and shared dialogue, critical reflection, and self-scrutiny. This includes on the part of the teacher as well as students. This open and relational model might also be related to Ward's broader cosmology and metaphysics.

PROCESS PHILOSOPHY AND COSMOLOGY

Ward's cosmology has been likened to process philosophy and theology, a similarity that in certain respects he acknowledges. For Ward, revelation involves a form of divine luring and guidance, in which God cooperates with humanity "within the limits of the culture of the day, being changed through a process of influence and influencing."[24] It is evident from this that God here is not posited as wholly impassable and atemporal. Whilst God embarks "in creation to realize specific purposes, God experiences that realization,"[25] offering a vision of the divine as dynamically imbricated with and affected by the historical process: a self-unfolding Mind that progressively expresses itself through a developing creation.

A personal idealist, Ward argues for a "synthesizing idea of a primordial consciousness that is ontologically prior to all physical realities . . . that produces emergent realities which can contribute to the sorts of value for the sake of which one possible universe may exist."[26] Such a universe hosts communities of finite minds, which are both self-developing and make new values possible. These societies are endowed with both creative freedom and moral responsibility, enabling free rational choice, autonomous self-organization, and an open, relational model of sociality.[27] This requires the rejection of closed and deterministic understandings of creation and cosmology. There is at the general level a purposiveness, but the system is sufficiently open for genuinely free, creative choice; the future envisaged acts as an influence "like a thought in the mind of the Creator which gives evolution a direction and goal."[28]

Ward makes reference to the seminal process philosopher Alfred North Whitehead. He recognizes that it was Whitehead who made the

24. Ward, *Religion and Revelation*, 109.
25. Potgieter, "Keith Ward's Soft Panentheism," 6.
26. Ward, *The Christian Idea of God*, 89.
27. Ward, *The Christian Idea of God*, 107.
28. Ward, *The Christian Idea of God*, 124.

concept of divine influence prominent rather than divine determination. He notes certain differences between process philosophy and his own views, rooted as they are in Christian orthodoxy, but nevertheless "as long as the ultimate sovereignty of God, the ultimate triumph of goodness, and the ultimate reality of finite persons is affirmed," he would not cavil at his work being termed a "process" view.[29] Accepting this designation, I would now like to pull out two significant strands of Ward's process view for pedagogy: love and creativity.

LOVE

Ward, in common with other Christian theologians and philosophers, lays emphasis on divine love. This is not only expressive of the nature of God; it is fundamental to God's creative, revelatory, and relational activity. It is also embedded in Ward's vision of cosmic teleology: though nature appears at times to be indifferent to the fate of the lives it generates, it can nevertheless be affirmed that the realization of partly self-shaped communities of love is the final goal of creation. Ward also considers whether holding that "God is love"[30] means that love, being essential to the divine nature, "can only be properly exercised in relation to others who are free to reciprocate love or not," and therefore creation of "some universe containing free finite agents" becomes an implication.[31] Within an orthodox Christian framework, the life of Jesus then becomes paradigmatic as the locus of divine self-giving love.

Teilhard de Chardin also centralized the significance of love. With some parallels to Ward, he saw love as "central to personal and social development, an essential source of human subjectivity and personal identity";[32] furthermore, this love, a cosmic energy, manifests in a dynamic, evolving universe. Love is not static. It is both dynamic and transformative, and translates into an active love for others. It involves "dependency and vulnerability, [consisting] of interrelationality, of enfolding, of helping the other, so that human flourishing can happen."[33] The implication is that centralizing God as love, love of God for humanity, and love of humanity for God involves centralizing love of humanity, in all places and situations,

---

29. Ward, *The Christian Idea of God*, 137, n. 3.
30. 1 John 4:16 (NRSV).
31. Ward, *The Christian Idea of God*, 196.
32. King, "Love Cosmic, Human and Divine," 178.
33. King, "Love Cosmic, Human and Divine," 181.

and in all our experiences and activities. This would include pedagogical practice. Strikingly pertinent here is Teilhard de Chardin's designation of love as "free and imaginative," an "outpouring of the spirit over all unexplored paths."[34] The resonances of all this with creative, open-ended, and relational pedagogical explorations are clear. So if love is at the heart of relationality and flourishing, what are the implications for pedagogy?

Despite a long history associating love with pedagogy, there can be some discomfort in contemplating practice in this sort of way. Cho identifies two forces at work here. The first, and obvious, source of potential unease is a tendency to link love with inappropriate and scandalous relations.[35] The second is the standardization movement, by which teachers "need only teach to the standards as impartially as possible," and the role of love, if it is even to exist in education, is reductively conceived as "motivating students to perform to the best of their abilities in the acquisition of knowledge," duly displayed via standardized tests.[36]

To take Cho's first point first, let us consider love as *eros*, as desire. Historically, this term has been used as both connected with but also distinct from human sexuality. Indeed, Plato related *eros* to the act of philosophy. Interpreting *eros* in this way, as also incorporating desire for beauty, truth, and wisdom, Hull argues for a model of education that, whilst fully acknowledging and cognizant of concerns about sexual harassment or exploitative teacher—student relations, nevertheless sees passion as a material force that can be harnessed in support of classroom experience. She comments:

> The inquiry I make here begins with my observation that too many students are dead in the water, bored, and lacking any real motivation to read, to study, to acquire knowledge. . . . These are signs of the sleep of desire. . . . Rather than gearing our teaching towards passing on to students some static bits of knowledge, I'd like to suggest a teaching model in which the object is to nurture the construction of a desiring self, a seeker of goals and goods and ends.[37]

Cho also argues that *eros* does have a place in the classroom, referencing bell hooks and her view that "an eroticized pedagogy does not mean a

34. Teilhard de Chardin, *The Future of Man*, 55.
35. Cho, "Lessons of Love," 125.
36. Cho, "Lessons of Love," 127.
37. Hull, "Eros and Education," 24.

sexualized pedagogy but one that is passionate and inspiring." However, the passion so incited goes beyond desire for knowledge for knowledge's sake and is instead transformative of the way a student looks upon the world. It thus carries the potential to challenge structures of domination and oppression.[38]

Seen in this way, *eros* in the classroom is not only a motivational force, inspiring students with intellectual passion for the pursuit of knowledge. It is a force that has the potential to restructure, perhaps radically, an individual's orientation towards the world. *Eros* may be not only indicative of a powerful force motivating growth and transformation, and involving "energy, suddenness, intensity, and beauty";[39] it may also be fundamentally disruptive. A passion for truth may interlock with a passion for justice, and a passion for justice may sit ill with instrumentalized models of education which depend on the inculcation of a pre-set slate of knowledge and skills deemed desirable by external authorities.

This speaks to Cho's rejection of the second force he sees as inimical to the notion of pedagogical love, the standardization movement. For he sees this in itself as a damaging phenomenon, promoting the reproduction rather than transformation of knowledge. Teaching, as Paulo Freire insists, cannot simply be "a process of transference of knowledge from the one teaching to the learner."[40] Citing Badiou and Lacan, Cho talks of love as "the name for a radical restructuring of a relation of two people . . . what Badiou means when he calls love a 'production of truth.'"[41] The love encounter between student and teacher, then, manifests as an enquiry into the world, not each other, an enquiry that takes place in partnership.

A further reason for reluctance to embrace the notion of pedagogical love is considered by Smith to emerge from a modernist mindset in which the personal must be sharply distinguished from the professional. Yet this distinction is seen to be false, unsustainable, and a "modernist conceit."[42] Expanding on this theme, one might further say that this depersonalization process reinforces relations of hierarchy through neutralization of the teacher as fellow human being and instead positing the teacher as a disembodied font of knowledge and authority. This undermines pedagogical

---

38. Cho, "Lessons of Love," 127.
39. Hull, "Eros and Education," 25.
40. Freire, *Teachers as Cultural Workers*, 22.
41. Cho, "Lessons of Love," 145.
42. Smith, "Love and the Child and Youth Care Relationship," 190.

trajectories that are in favor of conceiving the teacher–student relation as one of partnership and reciprocity. Such pedagogical trajectories, in turn, enable the empowerment of student voices and legitimation of their own location as producer and critic of knowledge. As Caraballo and Soleimany argue, this kind of "re-imagination of traditional roles of students and teachers" creates a space "where the multiple literacies and cultural specificities of marginalized students are acknowledged and valued."[43]

Pedagogical love thus functions as a spur towards practice that is inclined towards inclusivity, criticality, empowerment, and relationality. Speaking of school contexts, but equally aptly for higher education, Määttä and Uusiautti describe it as creating a setting where learners "can use and develop their own resources," individual circumstances are taken into consideration, and involving "persistent interest and perseverance" in the support of learners' development.[44]

Whilst affirming this, one may also sound a note of caution. Whether motivated by religious faith or not, I suggest that pedagogical love, and other forms of workplace love emerging through vocational commitment, might also need balancing with self-care and contextualized within workplace justice. It is all too easy for capitalist systems to systematically undervalue and exploit the contributions from carers, educators, community workers, healthcare workers, and the like. Nevertheless, it seems that the emphasis on love in relationality embedded in Ward's process cosmology may fruitfully be extended to pedagogical contexts. Let us now turn to the significance and place of creativity.

CREATIVITY

Ward's God, the cosmic Mind, is both "what it is by necessity," but also creatively free in relation to the contingent cosmos; the cosmos is posited as an "emergent, open, dialectical, relational organic unity,"[45] in which created finite minds are also creatively free. Again Ward acknowledges Whitehead as a forerunner in stressing the core value and significance of creativity (as in bringing something new into being). Whitehead proposed that each "actual occasion" or event drew from its past to project into the future through its own creative power. Ward endorses a cosmos with an open future in which

---

43. Caraballo and Soleimany, "In the Name of (Pedagogical) Love," 85.
44. Määttä and Uusiautti, "How to Raise Children to Be Good People?," 85.
45. Ward, *The Christian Idea of God*, 141.

such genuine creativity takes place as a perfection, not a defect detracting from the omnipotence and omniscience of God. He references here theologies and philosophies that see perfection as changeless contemplation of the Good,[46] contrasting this with views that place higher worth on the historical and particular as having intrinsic significance and not being effectively dispensable.[47]

For Ward's process view, in which the universe is becoming, evolving, and emergent, creativity is a great value and should be deemed a virtue.[48] This creativity is properly exercised in conjunction with other virtues such as appreciation and understanding of values such as truth, beauty and goodness, cooperation and compassion.

As Ward indicated, Whitehead also highlighted the significance of creativity. Whitehead's work has been specifically related to pedagogy, and he also wrote on education himself. I shall now reflect on some aspects of this as indicative of ways in which Ward's work might also underpin pedagogical theory and praxis.

Whitehead uses particular vocabulary. An actual entity (or occasion), as we have already seen, is an event. An eternal object is an entity that does not require specific reference to a particular actual entity—an abstraction, or possibility, one might say. For Whitehead, understanding actuality requires also apprehension of ideality—which includes unrealized potentials. Potentiality is realized in spatio-temporal actualization; this is concrescence into the determinate, the self-creation of the occasion.

Gershman and Oliver opine that it is not difficult to conceive of a student as actual entity, an education value as an eternal object, and intellectual growth as concrescence, whilst also accepting the occasional awkwardness in matching metaphysical categories to education: "We feel inclined to mention the 'actual entities' we had in Social Science 101 who showed no concrescence whatsoever, despite nine months of excellent instruction."[49] Yet they do find Whitehead's concept of creativity productive, in relation both to webs of relations within educational communities and a student's individual mind. It is offered up as pedagogically inspirational to conceive of learning as self-creation on the part of the student.[50]

46. Ward, *The Christian Idea of God*, 147.
47. Ward, *The Christian Idea of God*, 149.
48. Ward, *The Christian Idea of God*, 150.
49. Gershman and Oliver, "Towards a Process Pedagogy," 191.
50. Gershman and Oliver, "Towards a Process Pedagogy," 192.

This is not to be confused with stage-theorist understanding of "growth" in a serial manner. Being is becoming, and this is no less the case in pedagogical contexts. Becoming does not need to be planned and incremental; it is a self-impelled movement. Gershman and Oliver also critique educational perspectives that see the student as an object for improvement rather than a subject for self-development.

> The difference between improvement and movement has the same implications for education as the differences between the teacher's perspective and the student's perspective, between production and action, or between something which is administered and something which is sought.[51]

Active use of the student's own creativity is to be encouraged, with knowledge the catalyst for creativity—otherwise, knowledge is merely inert ideas. This was one of Whitehead's most crushing critiques of failing education. "Education with inert ideas is not only useless: it is, above all things, harmful."[52] This is by no means to say that education does not involve the teaching of knowledge. But such teaching recognizes the active involvement of the student. Education facilitates the process; it provides an appropriate level of structure, stimuli, and an appropriate environment. "The artist and the student are prototypes of Whitehead's actualization of potential: the individual apprehends, then manifests, his own data. No one accomplishes it for him, no one 'makes his own life' [Whitehead 1957, 57]."[53] Teachers are called on to see the student as a movement, engaging in a shared pursuit of knowledge.

This also requires the teacher to abandon the pretense of omnipotence. The so-called "sage on the stage" model has come under significant critique. It is especially associated with the pattern of the typical university lecture format. This is critiqued as promoting a transmission-based model of knowledge exchange, passive learning, and for exceeding optimal length to capture and keep audience attention—a form of critique we have already encountered in this paper. Education, says Whitehead, "is not a process of packing articles in a trunk. . . . Its nearest analogue is the assimilation of food by a living organism."[54] Active learning, as already mentioned, is

51. Gershman and Oliver, "Towards a Process Pedagogy," 193.

52. Whitehead, *Adventures of Ideas*, 1–2.

53. Gershman and Oliver, "Towards a Process Pedagogy," 57. The quotation is from Whitehead, *The Aims of Education and Other Essays*, 57.

54. Whitehead, *The Aims of Education and Other Essays*, 52.

increasingly recommended in contemporary pedagogical circles and may involve the so-called flipped classroom, whereby students undertake autonomous knowledge acquisition through engagement with provided materials such as texts and videos, and class time is spent on exploration, discussion, and problem solving.

Whitehead's liking for creativity and imagination in education led him (like Ward) to condemn dogmatism and the belief that one's ideas are "clear, obvious and irreformable."[55] Education instead ought to proceed holistically and rhythmically, inviting students to share in the "adventures of ideas";[56] the university, in particular, should be seen as a "learned and imaginative" way of living: "not an article of commerce."[57]

Whitehead is not without his critics, on a wide range of grounds. One I shall mention here as especially relevant is provided by Giarelli, in response to an article by Robert Roemer that compared the work of Whitehead and Paulo Freire, that leading light in critical pedagogy. One important point is that Whitehead's pedagogy is focused on the individual, unlike Freire's, which is fundamentally concerned with transformations of power relations and dialogic praxis. This key difference is also reflected in the almost total absence of the politics of oppression from Whitehead's pedagogical writings.[58] As Roemer says, "Freire explains bad pedagogy as a function of social imposition. Whitehead simply finds the human failing of laziness."[59] For Freire, oppression is manifested in political ontologies of difference, and the task is to disrupt these ontological differences through dialogue and love. To sum up:

> Whitehead bemoans the toiling millions and their discontent, as well as the unhappiness of their bosses, but offers a mystical ideal of a world where everyone can experience moments of intellectual joy. Roemer captures this difference neatly: Freire offers a pedagogy of the oppressed: Whitehead offers a pedagogy of the bored.[60]

It is true, as also argued by Tamboukou, that "power relations, capitalism and conflict were processes that he seems to have taken for granted,"[61] and

55. Whitehead, *Adventures of Ideas*, 223.
56. Whitehead, *Adventures of Ideas*, 259.
57. Whitehead, *The Aims of Education and Other Essays*, 97.
58. Giarelli, "Freire and Whitehead: Any Difference? Yes," 327.
59. Roemer, "Freire and Whitehead: Any Difference?," 320.
60. Giarelli, "Freire and Whitehead: Any Difference? Yes," 329.
61. Tamboukou, "Education as Action/the Adventure of Education," 143.

that transformation is presented on an individual basis, even whilst God is the "poet of the world, with tender patience leading it by his vision of truth, beauty and goodness."[62]

Taking this critique to Ward, it may be the case that his philosophy does not revolve around the questions from which social justice philosophers take their leave. However, it is ostensibly rooted in communities as well as being imbued with value in both the historical unfolding and the teleological vision of redemption. It also seeks to find "ways in which [we] can be positive and constructive forces in the contemporary project of constructing a consciously global society whose members can live in mutual understanding and co-operative action."[63]

Thus, Whitehead calls for a model of education that is dynamic, creative, to an extent open-ended, with students perceived as free entities pursuing knowledge and associated ideals of truth and value in nexuses of relations. I hope the analogies with Ward's process model are clear, and that this discussion of Whitehead illuminates further ways in which Ward's ideas may offer pedagogical inspiration.

CONCLUSION

This paper has sought to show that Ward's metaphysical account of personal idealism rooted in Christian faith may offer resources for and resonances with contemporary pedagogical models, particularly through his account of faith and reason in diverse contexts, and of process cosmology with its emphasis on dynamism, particularity, love, and creativity. If one supports core principles of Ward's account, this may constitute a philosophical and ethical imperative to resist instrumentalist and marketized models of education. I have also sought to show analogues between persons who hold faith positions and those who do not, who nevertheless are enmeshed in networks of attachments, commitments, ends, and values. In keeping with the spirit of comparative theology, I have sought insight in Ward's confessional account for a pedagogical model that may still resonate in secular contexts. This is most especially so if the fulfillment of human life is seen as the realization of values to which there is practical moral commitment, and those values include commitment to ideals such as goodness and justice.

62. Whitehead, *Process and Reality*, 346.
63. Ward, *Religion and Community*, 6.

BIBLIOGRAPHY

Aktas, Carla. "Enhancing Social Justice and Socially Just Pedagogy in Higher Education Through Participatory Action Research." *Teaching in Higher Education* 29.1 (2021) 159–75. https://doi.org/10.1080/13562517.2021.1966619.

Bartel, Timothy, ed. *Comparative Theology: Essays for Keith Ward*. London: SPCK, 2003.

Caraballo, Limarys, and Sahar Soleimany. "In the Name of (Pedagogical) Love: A Conceptual Framework for Transformative Teaching Grounded in Critical Youth Research." *The Urban Review* 51.1 (2019) 81–100. https://doi.org/10.1007/s11256-018-0486-5.

Cho, Daniel. "Lessons of Love: Psychoanalysis and Teacher–Student Love." *Educational Theory* 55.1 (2005) 79–96. https://doi.org/10.1111/j.1741-5446.2005.0006a.x.

Devlin, Keith. "Devlin's Angle: Most Math Problems Do Not Have a Unique Right Answer." *Devlin's Angle* (blog). August 1, 2014. http://devlinsangle.blogspot.com/2014/08/most-math-problems-do-not-have-unique.html.

Du Bois, W. E. B. *The Souls of Black Folk*. Chicago: McCurg, 1903. https://www.gutenberg.org/files/408/408-h/408-h.htm.

Fanon, Frantz. *Black Skin, White Masks*. New ed. London: Pluto, 1952.

Freire, Paulo. *Teachers as Cultural Workers: Letters to Those Who Dare Teach*. Boulder, CO: Westview, 1998.

Gershman, Kathleen, and Donald W. Oliver. "Towards a Process Pedagogy." *Process Studies* 16.3 (1987) 191–97. https://doi.org/10.2307/44798286.

Giarelli, James M. "Freire and Whitehead: Any Difference? Yes." *Philosophy of Education* (2006) 327–29.

Gordon, Lewis, ed. *Existence in Black: An Anthology of Black Existential Philosophy*. London: Routledge, 1996.

Hull, Kathleen. 2002. "Eros and Education: The Role of Desire in Teaching and Learning." *The NEA Higher Education Journal: Thought and Action* (Fall 2002) 19–32.

Kellaghan, Thomas, and Vincent Greaney. *Public Examinations Examined*. Washington, DC: World Bank, 2019. https://doi.org/10.1596/978-1-4648-1418-1.

King, Ursula. "Love Cosmic, Human and Divine: Pierre Teilhard de Chardin's Thoughts on the Phenomenon of Love." In *Comparative Theology: Essays for Keith Ward*, edited by T. W. Bartel, 177–87. London: SPCK, 2003.

Määttä, Kaarina, and Satu Uusiautti. "How to Raise Children to Be Good People?" *Analytic Teaching and Philosophical Praxis* 33.1 (2012) 83–91.

Neville, Robert Cummings. "Creation and Cosmology." In *Comparative Theology: Essays for Keith Ward*, edited by T. W. Bartel, 120–31. London: SPCK, 2003

Polkinghorne, John. "God, Science and Philosophy." In *Comparative Theology: Essays for Keith Ward*, edited by T. W. Bartel, 12–23. London: SPCK, 2003.

Potgieter, Raymond. "Keith Ward's Soft Panentheism." *Die Skriflig/In Luce Verbi* 47.1 (2013) 1–9.

Roemer, Robert E. "Freire and Whitehead: Any Difference?" *Philosophy of Education Yearbook* (December 2006) 318–26.

Sandel, Michael J. "The Procedural Republic and the Unencumbered Self." *Political Theory* 12.1 (1984) 81–96.

Sirvent, Roberto, and William Curtis Holtzen, eds. *By Faith and Reason: The Essential Keith Ward*. London: Darton, Longman and Todd, 2012.

Smith, Mark. "Love and the Child and Youth Care Relationship." *Relational Child and Youth Care Practice* 24.1–2 (2011) 189–92.

Tamboukou, Maria. "Education as Action/the Adventure of Education: Thinking with Arendt and Whitehead." *Journal of Educational Administration and History* 48.2 (2016) 136–47. https://doi.org/10.1080/00220620.2016.1144578.

Teilhard de Chardin, Pierre. *The Future of Man*. London: Collins, 1964.

Ward, Keith. *The Christian Idea of God: A Philosophical Foundation for Faith*. Cambridge: Cambridge University Press, 2017. https://doi.org/10.1017/9781108297431.

———. *Religion and Community*. Oxford: Clarendon, 2000.

———. *Religion and Revelation*. Oxford: Clarendon, 1994.

———. *Religion in the Modern World: Celebrating Pluralism and Diversity*. 1st ed. Cambridge: Cambridge University Press, 2019. https://doi.org/10.1017/9781108591997.

———. *What the Bible Really Teaches: A Challenge for Fundamentalists*. London: SPCK, 2004.

Watkins, C., and P. Mortimer. "Pedagogy: What Do We Know?" In *Understanding Pedagogy and Its Impact on Learning*, edited by P. Mortimer, 1–19. London: Chapman/Sage, 1999.

Whitehead, Alfred North. *Adventures of Ideas*. New York: Free, 1967.

———. *The Aims of Education and Other Essays*. New York: Free, 1957.

———. *Process and Reality: An Essay in Cosmology*. Edited by David Ray Griffin and Donald W. Sherburne. Gifford Lectures, 1927–28. New York: Free, 1978.

Keith Ward's Response to J'annine Jobling

J'ANNINE IS RIGHT IN saying that I have rarely written explicitly about pedagogy and I am very grateful to her for spelling out some implications she sees in my work for the theory of education. I wholly agree with what she has said about education, and I am pleased that she sees my work as in harmony with her own.

I thought what I would do in response is to say something about the teaching of theology and religion in schools and colleges, thinking that it would apply to the teaching of philosophy and other humanities subjects too.

This is unfortunately a time when disinformation, prejudice, and hatred are commonly expressed in social media, when it has become acceptable to describe views other than one's own in negative terms that proponents of those views would not accept, and when there is a real possibility of social unrest arising from misunderstanding of others.

In such a time, it is vital that just appreciation, critical thinking, and informed understanding should be seen as vital aims of any true education. The study of philosophy, and of theology and religion, is particularly well suited to realize such aims, as attitudes to basic philosophical and religious ideas underlie many of the issues that are often subject to misunderstanding and ignorance, and can then be potentially disruptive in society.

What I have to say applies to both philosophy and theology, but as this book is mostly about theology, I will concentrate on the latter. Theology used to be seen as the articulation and defense of the beliefs and practices of a specific religion, usually Christianity. In some quarters, it is still seen in that way. But as universities and schools have become increasingly secular, and as greater knowledge of the world's diverse religions has grown, it has become clear to many that the study of *theos*, of God, should involve a study of the many different views of God that exist.

God and Faith

Even within Christianity there are very different concepts of God, ranging from the *esse suum subsistens* of Thomistic thought to the "sufferer who understands" of process theology, and the "Absolute Spirit" of Hegelian idealism. But cast the net wider, and it becomes clear that many religions, not all of which use the word "God," have ideas of a supreme spiritual reality and that such ideas underlie discernibly religious practices.

So it becomes possible to speak of a wider notion of theology as the study of ideas of a supreme, or at least other and greater than human, spiritual reality. The advantage is that one will be able to place the beliefs with which one is familiar in a wider historical context, and to expand the range of human thought about such matters beyond the rather limited confines of one's most familiar environment. The disadvantage is that one may get lost in a vast sea of possibilities, which no one could master in a lifetime.

The same could be said, of course, of any study of history or of the sciences, and so there is a need to specialize in some particular areas of thought, and not try to cover everything. Nevertheless, getting some idea of the general range of human thought about alleged spiritual realities, however relatively superficial and over-general it may be—and it will be important to admit a degree of superficiality—is an important way of seeing the wider context of the leading ideas of one's own time and place.

I am convinced that it is not true that all one needs to understand religion is contained already in the Christian tradition, and that there is nothing to learn both from other traditions and from secular and scientific thought. On the contrary, I agree with Max Muller that he who knows only one religion knows none.

What distinguishes comparative theology, in my view, is that it studies particular religious traditions in the light of a wider set of such traditions, which may better illuminate both its strengths and weaknesses. It does not seek to defend a specific tradition (though individual teachers, of course, may defend their own beliefs, without requiring that others agree with them). Like old-style confessional theology, it covers many disciplines—the analysis of texts, historical and social influences, philosophical presuppositions, and the development of beliefs and practices. Its distinctive method is to do so with explicit reference to the global and historical context of religious beliefs. This requires comparison, not to find a winner, but to expand critical and appreciative understanding of the nature of human beliefs about God, the gods, or the existence of a spiritual dimension to reality.

Whatever such a course is called, it should be, and in many cases already is, an important part of learning and research in the humanities. The deepening of understanding, the practices of critical and judicious thinking, and the widening of perspectives that it should provide is in itself a great good. And its contribution to a society that is increasingly diverse could be of immense importance. For it is better to have an informed and discriminating body of people than one that relies for knowledge on prejudice and hearsay. For these reasons, I believe it is important that the teaching of theology, and of philosophy too, in a global sense, should be a central part of any education that seeks not merely to provide information, but to train the mind in practical and humane wisdom.

DISCUSSION QUESTIONS

1. How does Ward's theology align with or diverge from Freire's model of liberatory education? Should theological education be more explicitly geared toward social justice and transformation?

2. Should theological education adopt a more flexible model of learning, allowing students to explore theology in non-structured ways? What dangers might arise from excessive ambiguity in academic settings?

3. Should theological institutions require comparative theology as a core component of training? What are the risks and rewards of introducing comparative religious studies in Christian seminaries?

4. Ward affirms that "he who knows only one religion knows none." In what ways does this approach support or challenge traditional Christian pedagogy?

5. Does process thought necessarily imply a particular model of educational pedagogy? If so, what would that pedagogy look like in practice, and how might it differ from traditional models of instruction?

6

Possibility, Value, and Mind
The Entangled Heart of Keith Ward's Philosophical Theology

ANDREW M. DAVIS

For decades Keith Ward has lifted his readers' gaze to an idealist view of life over and above the malaise of materialism and its many discontents.[1] Having had his own philosophical training in the British empiricist tradition, Ward has consistently prioritized experience, consciousness, and value and opposed their reductive negation in materialistic explanations of human existence, experience, and the cosmos at large. As Ward has expressed it, philosophical idealism holds that Mind is the only ontological primitive and the entire cosmos is its product.[2] The physical universe cannot exist without Mind and its deepest nature is that it is an expressive appearance of Mind and its contents. Ward's long-held advocacy of *personal idealism* in particular holds that the reality of cosmic Mind consists in knowing, thinking, feeling, and intending.[3]

---

1. See for example Ward, *More Than Matter?*, ch. 14; and Ward, *God and the Philosophers*, ch. 11.

2. Ward, *The Christian Idea of God*, 9. In this chapter, I will follow Ward's own capitalization of "Mind" to indicate its distinction from any finite mind. See Ward, *Priority of Mind*, 35. Where relevant, I will also capitalize "Possibility," "Value," "Goodness," and other terms to indicate their preeminent or necessary status in the nature of things.

3. Ward, *The Christian Idea of God*, 1, 9. For a personal overview of Ward's own philosophical and religious journey, see Ward, "My Journey to the God of Personal Idealism." For Ward's discussion of distinctions between absolute and personal idealism, refer to Ward, *Morality, Autonomy and God*, ch. 14.

POSSIBILITY, VALUE, AND MIND

The metaphysical backdrop to human existence and experience, therefore, is not impersonal, unconscious, or valueless for Ward, but deeply personal, supremely conscious, and of ultimate intrinsic worth. As I've recently argued, Ward belongs securely within the *axianoetic* tradition of Western philosophical theology wherein both Value (Gk. *axia*) and Mind (Gk. *noētikos*) are affirmed as ultimate in the nature of things. "Somehow," Ward states, "the factors of consciousness and value must be included in any comprehensive account of Ultimate Reality."[4] As to precisely how Mind and Value should be included or related to each other in approaching ultimacy, however, has remained a debate throughout the axioanetoic tradition, with different distinctions, emphases, and priorities available.[5]

In holding to the "priority of Mind," Ward can incorporate not only a *nomological* explanation of the universe in terms of the physical and law-like domains of natural science, but also an *axiological* explanation so that intentional, purposive, and evaluative dimensions of existence actually have a place. It remains a fundamental conviction for Ward: without Mind, Value dissolves. Moreover, it is in the context of primordial Mind that a "principle of axiology" could actually apply to the entire universe. A purposeful explanation in terms of Value could provide an explanation of why the universe as such exists.[6] Supposing a necessary "array of possible states, with the values they necessarily have," there would then be "an intrinsic reason for the existence of any universe—namely, the goodness that it would exhibit." Its intrinsic worth for Ward would give it a "wholly satisfactory" axiological explanation, and thus justify its actualization by an ultimate Mind.[7] Deeper still, Ward claims that an axiological explanation in terms of ultimate intrinsic worth would also adequately explain the necessary existence of this Mind and thus also its necessary production of a worthwhile cosmos. "If you say that something is just worth existing for its own sake . . . you have answered the question, 'Why does it exist?'" Ward states. "To say that something is valuable is a question-stopping

---

4. Ward, *The Big Questions in Science and Religion*, 242.

5. The roots of the axianoetic tradition date back to the genius of Plato and Aristotle and are differently inherited and employed by key figures throughout Western philosophical and theological history. These include a variety of ancient, medieval, and modern thinkers, including Plotinus, Anselm, Aquinas, Descartes, Leibniz, Spinoza, Hegel, Whitehead, A. C. Ewing, John Leslie, Peter Forrest, Keith Ward, John Polkinghorne, among others. See Davis, *Mind, Value and Cosmos*.

6. Ward, *The Evidence for God*, 72, 51.

7. Ward, *The Christian Idea of God*, 97.

explanation, probably the only question-stopping explanation that really works."[8] It is thus not only Mind, but also Value that lies at the explanatory depths of both God and the world.

In appreciation of these profound layers of Ward's axianoetic metaphysics, my goal in this chapter is to peel them back more fully so that readers might appreciate (at least in part) how Ward has progressively reached these conclusions. In particular, I aim to demonstrate how Ward has arrived at personal idealism through a lively ontological wrestle with Possibility, Value, and Mind and a host of questions and challenges concerning them, including implications for the God–world relationship. Where relevant, I will point to elements of vagueness in Ward's proposal and raise some critical questions of my own. I remain deeply indebted to Ward's vision and the playful spirit with which he approaches questions of ultimate concern. My hope is that his subsequent readers will continue to wrestle with Possibility, Value, and Mind as the entangled heart of his philosophical theology.

THE ABYSS OF POSSIBILITY

For anything to exist in actuality presupposes its "existence" in possibility. Before your actual existence, for example, your possibility was *there* in the nature of things. Even throughout your existence your possibility remains beside you like a haunting metaphysical shadow. But *where* is the intricacy of your possibility and *how* can it "exist" prior to your actual existence? Deeper still: *why* are any possibilities actualized at all? Such questions are not merely posed of yourself but also of the entire universe of which you are a part.

Affirming and problematizing the ontological abyss of possibility has been central throughout Keith Ward's corpus. For Ward, we can and perhaps must hold to the necessary reality of a "complete array of every possibility of any kind, something like the Platonic world of Forms."[9] One need not reproduce Plato and reify or essentialize this realm as "independent," "higher," or "more real" in comparison to actuality, however.[10] Neither should they simply dismiss it as non-existent. Rather, the Platonic world

---

8. Ward, *The Priority of Mind*, 46.

9. Ward, *Pascal's Fire*, 131.

10. "What goes wrong with the Platonic world," Ward rightly states, "is that the forms are seen as the eminent and truly real world, and the world of sense-experience, of personal relationships, of beer and skittles and suffering and love is demoted to a shadowy half-reality." Ward, *God, Chance, Necessity*, 29.

provides the intelligible archetypes, structures, patterns, and relationships presupposed not simply by our existence and the actual universe but also by an infinitude of other possible universes. Indeed, the fundamental elements of our actual universe, Ward states, are governed by a limited subset of mathematically pictured "Platonic possibilities." He likens these to the abstract "skeleton" or "map" of the universe, but is quick to remind us that "skeletons are not living forms, and maps are not landscapes in which one can breathe and walk"—these are abstractions.[11]

Possibilities are abstract and not actual, but they nevertheless *do* "exist." Even if there were no actual universe, "its possibility would exist, together with the possibilities of every other possible universe, all comprising an infinite set of possibilities," Ward states.[12] If something is ever truly *possible* (existing in *one possible world*), then it must always be possible. In this way, Ward insists that "the complete array of possibles cannot be thought away in any world."[13] Put differently: "if a thing is ever possible, surely it is always possible. That is, if it is ever true that x may be the case, then it must be always and immutably true that x may be the case, under suitably specified conditions."[14] Thus, the Platonic abyss of possibility is deep both with *infinitude* and also *necessity*.

Peering still deeper into the abyss of possibilities, Ward draws our attention to the fact that possibilities are not neutral or vacuous in nature, but exhibit a real *axiological depth*. Possibilities come tangled with a certain objective *value-character* that we all inevitably presuppose. We do not simply *impose* this axiological character, but find it *given* with existence and its myriad possibilities: all that *might have been* in the past; all that *currently is* in the present; and all that *still may be* in the future. Consider the infinite possible ways our world might have been different on a total scale; or the infinite possibilities or forms of all species that may or may not have emerged on our planet; or all the possible historical trajectories that might have been and still may be on this pale blue dot. Are these possibilities axiologically vacuous? Are not *better* and *worse* really applicable to this infinite spectrum of possibility?

Ward answers in the affirmative: the necessary realm of possibility retains the values they necessarily have and there can be a goodness or

---

11. Ward, *God, Chance, Necessity*, 29.
12. Ward, *God, Chance, Necessity*, 36.
13. Ward, *Religion and Creation*, 196.
14. Ward, *Rational Theology and the Creativity of God*, 153.

intrinsic value to possibilities that is necessarily what it is, just as there can be a badness or objective disvalue associated with their opposites.[15] For example, is the trajectory of our planet toward ecocide and the eradication of all species? Or, is there a sustainable path forward toward the harmony and wellbeing of possums, people, and the planet? These are not neutral possibilities: ecological harmony really is *better* than ecocide. Will human relations be destroyed by political idiocy, division, and hatred? Or, is there a way beyond partisan divides and extremism? These are not neutral possibilities either: division and hatred really are *worse* than unity and love. These better and worse paths involve live and weighty possibilities; they form the wavering and risky horizon of the future where tragedy and triumph are real possibilities. Put simply: for Ward, the abyss of possibility is also an abyss of *Value*.

PROBLEMATIZING THE ABYSS

While the reality of such an infinite, necessary and value-laden abyss seems far from absurd for Ward, he fully recognizes that it is not unproblematic metaphysically. No honest philosopher can look into this abyss and walk away without a sense of haunting. Modifying Nietzsche: *When you gaze into the abyss the abyss gazes back at you in the form of your own possibility and value*.[16] Throughout his work, Ward has problematized the ontological status of possibilities, saying "It may seem rather odd . . . to think of a 'complete array of all possible states.' In what sense would such a thing exist? Things, it may be said, are either actual or non-existent," he states, but "there cannot be actually existent possibles."[17] A fundamental question thus rises from the abyss for Ward: "[H]ow can mere possibilities exist?"[18] He readily grants that the "existence" of possibilities may be an objectionable thesis. Some will no doubt insist that possibilities cannot and do not "exist"; they are just "useful fictions." Ward, however, holds firm: "the Platonic reminiscence continues to haunt us," he states, "the possibility of things is not a mere non-being. It has a potentiality to be. It has some form of existence. If so, it must have some form of actuality." The abyss of possibilities—what Boethius calls the "infinite ocean of being"—harbors "all

---

15. Ward, *The Christian Idea of God*, 97.
16. Refer to Nietzsche, *Beyond Good and Evil*, ch. 4.
17. Ward, *The Christian Idea of God*, 93.
18. Ward, *God, Chance, Necessity*, 36.

potentialities for being," but "not as actual, and yet not as simple nullities."[19] Possibilities for Ward should thus be *distinguished* from absolute nothingness and can scarcely just "exist" in some pseudo-real world between Being and Nothingness. "Possibilities cannot simply exist unsupported in a half-real world between non-being and actual-being," he states. "Half-existence is not good enough; you either exist or you do not. Yet it makes sense to speak of possible existences, of real potentialities, that are different from absolute nothingness."[20]

In problematizing the ontological status of possibilities, Ward points not only to the question of *how* possibilities as such can "exist," but also to the question of *why* "any possibility should be actualized at all."[21] Why, indeed? In the face of infinite possibilities and infinite possible universes, some limiting principle and/or criterion of selection and actualization must be operative. It thus remains for Ward a "major problem" not only to consider the "sense in which such possible worlds really exist," but also "how some (or all?) of them get 'selected' for actuality."[22] For Ward, these are bedrock ontological questions that cannot be avoided by any adequate metaphysics.

ACTUALITY, LOGICAL NECESSITY, AND MIND

How does one begin to approach such abysmal metaphysical questions? Drawing from the wisdom of the past, Ward has consistently put forth a "Platonic-Augustinian" model to address the ontological challenges posed by the abyss of possibility.[23] At the heart of this approach is the explanatory force he finds expressed in that "ancient saying" that "anything actual must either be caused by something actual and with at least as much actuality as it has, or be such that it could not possibly be caused by anything."[24] Alongside an entire current of western philosophical theology, Aquinas inherited this Aristotelian tradition and put it succinctly: "Actual existence takes

---

19. Ward, *Religion and Creation*, 197.
20. Ward, *God, Chance, Necessity*, 48.
21. Ward, *God, Chance, Necessity*, 47.
22. Ward, *Pascal's Fire*, 38.
23. This is found to be the case not only in *Rational Theology and the Creativity of God* published in 1982, but also in *The Christian Idea of God* recently published in 2017.
24. Ward, *God, Chance, Necessity*, 48.

precedence of potential existence."[25] This statement for Ward is not a denial of possibility, but an affirmation of its *necessary weddedness to actuality*. Recall that one of the principal challenges of the abyss of possibility is its very "existence"—and its *necessary* existence at that. In *what sense* would a necessary "array of all possible states" plausibly "exist"—and *how*? If, for example, our "laws of nature" are but a set of many possible laws, then a clear problem presents itself as to the ontological status and nature of those laws. "Do they really exist," Ward asks, "and if so, where? How can one be sure they will continue to apply to nature?" Why these laws and not others anyway?[26]

One may naturally try to run from such questions, but the Platonic abyss still haunts. Avoiding them is like trying to run from your shadow on a sunlit day. Neither is it helpful for Ward to leave such possibilities unintegrated—as Plato arguably did—floating in some sky-like metaphysical void. If possibilities "exist" at all, they must, in virtue of the "ancient saying," have *subsistent* dependence upon something actual. Ward is adamant that we "must be logically ruthless, and say that either there are really no possibilities or that they exist in something actual."[27] It seems obvious that it is not *possible* to deny the reality of possibility without assuming its reality. Human existence and experience presuppose this. On Ward's account then, we are continually forced toward *actuality as inclusive of possibility*. But in order to include the abyss of possibility, this actuality must also match its *necessity*.

As Ward has stressed, this necessary actuality would be *the ground* of possibility—that without which nothing at all is possible.[28] Put differently, it would be an actuality "which exists in every possible logical world (where 'a world' is taken to cover absolutely everything that actually exists)." If anything at all is ever possible, then there exists an actuality that includes that possibility, and if that actuality is the same in all possible worlds, then by definition that actuality is *necessary*.[29] Put still differently, this actuality would be the only thing that must be *actual* if anything at all is *possible*, and

---

25. Ward, *Rational Theology and the Creativity of God*, 35; Ward, *Christian Idea of God*, 93; Ward, *Sharing in the Divine Nature*, 84.

26. Ward, *God, Chance, Necessity*, 53–54. For a stimulating collection rethinking the laws of nature as dynamic and emergent, see Cartwright and Ward, *Rethinking Order*.

27. Ward, *God, Chance, Necessity*, 36.

28. Ward, *Rational Theology and the Creativity of God*, 35

29. Ward, *God, Chance, Necessity*, 36.

there cannot be any possible alternatives to it because it is the *condition of the possibility of alternatives*.[30] Should one agree to the plausibility of the "ancient saying," then a natural question results: What is (or must) this actuality be in order to include the infinitude of abstract, non-physical possibility within itself? Ward answers with analogical wisdom: it is a Mind, an ultimate and necessary Mind that is the "actual basis of all possible states."[31] Possibilities therefore do not "exist" in a void, but *subsist* in a Mind. The abyss of possibility is also an abyss of *Mind* and possibilities are its contents.

In holding to the necessary reality of the possible, Ward rightly insists that he has put forth a "basically Platonic" vision, one that has been revived in a variety of proposals in recent years, not least in those of John Leslie, Roger Penrose, and others.[32] Yet in contrast to these thinkers, he has repeatedly stressed the *integrative value* of Augustine's Middle Platonic move as a necessary complement to the Platonic vision of "Forms" or "Ideas." "It was Augustine who formulated an elegant integration between these elements by placing the world of the Forms in the mind of the primordial intellect, and making the physical cosmos a 'moving image of eternity,' a world selected by intellect out of the world of Forms . . . ."[33]

This move for Ward is of no small consequence: it eases "the problem of what it could mean to speak of the actual existence of a mere possibility; for their actuality becomes that of the mind in which they inhere."[34] Ward thus follows the Middle Platonic tradition in holding that it is Mind or Consciousness that "stores possibilities non-physically and mind that can act for a reason—that is, in order to make actual some possible states." The natural result of this conviction is that Mind is "a fundamental constituent of ultimate reality and is necessarily prior to all physical entities." Such states are actualizations of possibilities apprehended by cosmic Mind, which is "the only actuality that is not capable of being brought into being or of not existing or of being other than it is, precisely because it is a condition of the existence of any possibilities whatsoever." "Cosmic consciousness," Ward concludes, "is the condition of any and all possibilities existing

---

30. Ward, *Pascal's Fire*, 132.

31. Ward, *Pascal's Fire*, 132.

32. See for example, Ward, *Christ and the Cosmos*, 188–90; Ward, *God, Chance, Necessity*, 22, 43–44; Ward, *Big Questions in Science and Religion*, 26; Ward, *Christian Idea of God*, 84; Ward, *The Priority of Mind*, 81.

33. Ward, *Morality, Autonomy and God*, 107–8.

34. Ward, *Rational Theology and the Creativity of God*, 153.

... and not merely a very complex thing that just happens to exist."[35] While this makes compelling sense logically, one might still be moved to ask *why* such a Mind and its contents should exist in the first place? What is it that reasons or explains this Mind beyond the claim that it is the actual condition of any and all possibilities? This is a question about the nature of *divine necessity* and it is (arguably) deeper than the ontological problem of possibility that this Mind (arguably) resolves. Here Ward moves from *logical* considerations to *axiological* convictions.

AXIANOETIC NECESSITY AND MUTUAL IMMANENCE

Let's recall that for Ward possibilities are not empty of content and character, but come suffused with necessary values. All possibilities are possibilities of greater and lesser value, and the cosmic Mind in which they inhere includes all of them: the good, the bad, and the ugly. Possibility and Value for Ward must be integrated into Mind because it is Mind that *thinks* possibilities and *evaluates* them in terms of their objective or intrinsic worth. Possibilities of value are dependent upon the thoughts and evaluation of this Mind, but is this Mind dependent upon nothing at all? What accounts for its necessity? As the tradition has said, a *necessary* Mind depends upon nothing other than itself in order to exist. It exists in and through itself such that its own existence is *eternally self-sustaining*. But what can possibly clarify this bewildering idea? It is not enough to say this Mind is just a "brute fact that is inexplicable," as Richard Swinburne once put it (and Ward rightly critiqued); nor does it help to point to ultimate mystery.[36] For Ward, this really is a serious issue: either this Mind cannot be accounted for—"which makes its existence something which just happens to be the case"—or it somehow accounts for its own existence.[37]

In approaching this abysmal question, it may help to remember that whatever is actual is also possible (otherwise it wouldn't be actual). This must also apply to the necessity of primordial Mind. If, according to Ward, all possibilities are necessarily wedded to this Mind's actuality, this *must* also include this Mind's *own possibility*. As Ward has reiterated, it would have to uniquely be the case that necessary Mind "is actual *both* as possibility *and*

---

35. Ward, *Christian Idea of God*, 98.

36. For Ward's critique of Swinburne, See Ward, *Rational Theology and the Creativity of God*, 93–99.

37. Ward, *Religion and Creation*, 195.

as instantiated."[38] Now if every possibility has its necessary value, a natural question emerges: What is the value of this cosmic Mind's own possibility? Is it not the *ultimate intrinsic Value*—the very Possibility of all possibilities? And does not this possibility as necessarily "instantiated" (actualized) make this Mind the supreme and unsurpassable Value—indeed, the Actuality of all actualities and the Value of all values? This is a thought experiment that resonates with what Ward once referred to as Anselm's "absolutely infuriating" influence, and it has remained controversial throughout the history of philosophical theology.[39]

Rising from the abyss, these tangled questions are followed by yet another that is eminently worth posing: *Is not the intrinsic value or goodness of something a reason for its existence?* Put differently, could this Mind exist precisely because of its *Goodness*—because it is *supremely good that it should?* As Ward has communicated, an "axiological explanation" concerning intrinsic value seems to be "the only question-stopping explanation that really works"—and it might even work for God.[40] Rather than being some kind of axiological magic, this conviction has deep and abiding roots in the western philosophical tradition.

Plato famously set at the apex of reality a mysterious "thing that every soul pursues as the end of all her action, dimly divining its existence, but perplexed and unable to grasp its nature." This is the Form of the Good and the "highest object of knowledge." The Good is "beyond being" for Plato, but that through which "everything that is good and right derives its value." For Ward this is an "unmistakable adumbration" of the abstract God of the philosophers, but he reminds us that Plato says little more of this "ultimate cause and object of intellectual knowledge."[41]

The Good for Plato constitutes the ultimate axiological reason, explanation or requirement for being. Ward agrees, but again stresses that it is unclear how anything as abstract as the "Good" could "exist," let alone *do* anything. After all, abstractions are by definition *causally inert*. For Ward, an objective framework of Value or Goodness in the universe thus seems to *require* embedding within some kind of primordial Mentality or Consciousness. This is not apparent in Plato, but Ward rightly suggests that the "addition of Mind to the Good" would provide an ultimate axiology reason

38. Personal correspondence, my emphasis.
39. Ward, *God: A Guide for the Perplexed*, 127.
40. Ward, *Priority of Mind*, 46–47.
41. Ward, *Rational Theology*, 211–12.

for this Mind as an ultimate intrinsic Value. In part, this was the move of Aristotle, who closed "the gap" between Plato's Demiurge and the Good with a *Mind* that eternally thinks itself (*noesis noeseos*). "But if there is something which, as Aristotle has suggested, cannot exist otherwise than as it does, the best reason for its existence would lie in its supreme goodness," Ward states. "To be rationally explicable, it has to contain the reason for its existence in itself. So a rationally explicable being is a necessary being which is supremely good." Ward continues: "A supremely good necessary being is ultimately explanatory in that it necessarily desires its own existence as that which is most worthy of existence."[42] That this "being" is a *thinking being*—a Mind—seems to be a necessary condition of its Goodness.

Although Ward stresses the "priority of Mind," he also vaguely recognizes some manner of *inherent relationality* between Mind *and* Value. The best explanation for Mind is that it is supremely valuable, "not least to itself," he states.[43] This is an implicit recognition of *distinction* and *relationality* between Value and Mind such that Mind's existence is explained not only in terms of its *Goodness*, but also in terms of its *knowledge or awareness* of this Goodness. There are two relations here: *from Value to Mind* and *from Mind to Value*; they can be distinguished, but not fully isolated from the other in the necessary life of God. From one direction, the weddedness of *Mind* to the Good provides the Good with the only context in which *axiological reasons* can be given, namely, that of Mind (*noētikos*). From the other direction, the weddedness of the *Good* to the Mind provides this Mind with an ultimate reason for existing, namely, its supreme intrinsic Value (*axia*). There is thus a mutual provision between Value and Mind that is really there in Ward's approach to divine necessity. There is equally a mutual provision between *possibility* and *actuality* in the life of God. It is, therefore, not only the "priority of Mind" that Ward offers his readers as a philosophical idealist, but more so the *priority of relationality* as a truly *axianoetic* thinker. From this perspective, the mystery of divine necessity lies in what Whitehead calls the "mutual immanence" of the divine life, where *Possibility, Value, Actuality,* and *Mind* all coincide in perichoretic union.[44]

---

42. Ward, *Religion and Creation*, 196.
43. Ward, *Religion and Creation*.
44. Refer to Davis, *Mind, Value and Cosmos*; and Ward, *Christ and the Cosmos*, ch. 36.

DIVINE LIMITATION AND WORLDLY PERSUASION

There is much that follows from this relational approach that Ward finds significant for thinking about the God–world relationship and why there is a world (or worlds) at all. In the first place, if the divine Mind is the omniscient ground of the possible, such that possibilities are contents of divine knowledge, then Ward stresses that it will also have "the creative power to make thoughts actual." This connection between *knowledge of possibilities* and the *ability to actualize them* seems a coherent one. For Ward, there must be a "power" able to actualize possibilities "because if something is possible, that means that it *could exist*. Some power must be able to make it exist, or it would not really be *possible*, and a reality which itself actually exists by necessity would possess in its own nature the power of existence." It is this power, for Ward, "which could bring possibilities into actuality."[45]

One of the necessary corollaries of holding that it is the intrinsic Value or Goodness of the divine Mind that reasons its existence is that this Mind is necessarily *constrained* by Goodness. "God's power is limited by God's goodness," Ward states.[46] To be the ground of all possibility and to be Good requires that *not every possibility* be pursued for actualization. After all, many possibilities are evil and thus not worth actualizing in and for themselves. In attempting to make sense of the existence of *our world*, Ward therefore rightly stresses that one of the "most repugnant" aspects of some "many worlds" theories is that *every possibility* (every possible world) is necessarily actualized somewhere without any selecting or limiting factor whatsoever. This would be a truly hellish abyss as Ward rightly communicates. Where there is no axiological limit on the possible, "there must exist universes that are totally morally repugnant, in which sentient beings are totally irrational and in which they all suffer unending and excruciating torments for no reason . . . ." "In such a system," Ward states, "there would not just be one Hell, which would be bad enough. There would be an endless series of Hells, each bad in its own way."[47]

However, if *Mind* is the only context in which necessary possibilities can be explained, and if *Value* or *Goodness* is the only context in which this Mind can be explained, then the selective capacities of this Mind will be inherently limited by Value. "If the creator has any decency," Ward insists,

---

45. Ward, *Christian Idea of God*, 127–28 (emphasis added).
46. Ward, *Sharing in the Divine Nature*, 112–13.
47. Ward, *Pascal's Fire*, 137–38.

"the possibly enormous set of extremely bad universes, in which there is endless and totally pointless suffering, will not be actualized. Some selection between possible universes will be needed." The criterion of selecting possibilities is precisely that of Value: "If possibilities exist in the mind of God" Ward continues, "then only those possibilities will be actualized that exhibit some preponderance of value" so that each "actual universe will retain its own unique distinctive value."[48] What is more, Ward again follows Augustine in having no qualms about a "principle of plenitude" as an essential characteristic of primordial Mentality. This principle would hold "that it is good that every possible sort of good should exist, as long as its existence does not come at the price of excessive and pointless harm." "Perhaps there is something in the divine nature that causes it to generate many possible sorts of goods, even though some kinds will inevitably incur suffering."[49] For Ward, this "something" in the divine nature is the supremacy of Value and its plenitudinous expression in this, and perhaps many worthwhile worlds.

Now if God is limited by God's goodness, only actualizing worthwhile possibilities, it follows directly that a world such as ours exists because it is *good that it should*. This may come as a shock to Schopenhauerian pessimists who cannot help but see our world as one of the many hells Ward spoke of above.[50] Yet it seems obvious that ours is not an utterly hellish world, but a world of competing values and disvalues. Neither is the claim that our world exists because it is *worth existing* the claim that ours is the "best possible world." Here, Ward follows Aquinas rather than Leibniz in strongly doubting that there is only one "best possible" world. Instead, he points to the likelihood that there are many possible worlds exhibiting various forms of goodness without any one of them being "absolutely the best."[51] One might very well suppose that if the divine Mind is both omnipotent *and* Good then it *must* produce the absolutely best possible world without fail; but since it strains credulity to claim that our world is the absolute best, then such a divine Mind is not good, or is not omnipotent, or simply does not exist!

---

48. Ward, *Pascal's Fire*, 138.

49. Ward, *Pascal's Fire*. For Ward's recent discussion of the "principle of plenitude" see Ward, *Religion in the Modern World*, ch. 13.

50. See Ward, *Rational Theology*, 70; Ward, *Guide for the Perplexed*, 225–26.

51. Ward, *Pascal's Fire*, 134.

For Ward, part of what it means for God's power to be limited by Goodness is that divine activity and creativity are *necessarily persuasive* rather than all-controlling or all-determining. Ward stresses that "creation" does not mean "determiner in all respects"; rather, God is a "contributory cause," offering a "teleological impetus to the world" while leaving the actualization of this impetus to the "complex of finite agencies."[52] Put differently: God is in the business of creating a *self-creating* world. Ward has thus been a critic of unlimited omnipotence and credits Alfred North Whitehead and Stewart Sutherland for convincing him "that the notion of omnipotence needed to be reformulated, and the idea of human freedom and creativity needed to be more clearly emphasized."[53] It is the necessary limitation of divine power by divine Goodness that allows for the real value of otherness, relationship, freedom, and self-creation in the world.

LOVE, NECESSARY CREATION, AND CULMINATION

Ward fully realizes that a divine Mind conceived in terms of supreme Goodness seems *destined* to have a creation. Is it not the nature of Value or the Good to *necessarily diffuse* itself as the philosophical tradition has long insisted? What if this supreme Value is conceived as *Love*? It is this distinctively Christian insight that Ward affirms: "the supreme value is ecstatic love, an overflowing of being to share value." This means that God cannot be conceived as some kind of "impersonal substance" or "blind force of compulsion" which necessarily emanates an inevitable and unwilled creation (somewhat like the Neoplatonic vision of the Many emanating from the One). God will rather be a "personal being of love and freedom," who necessarily affirms the divine existence as of supreme value" by willing a worldly other into being and relationship.[54] Ward recognizes that the particular Christian insistence that "God is Love" (1 John 4:16) requires a God who does not remain isolated in the contemplation of all things good and beautiful as merely possible within itself. He is right to say that "this seems to commit one to the belief that God *must* create a universe of finite persons, as a condition of realizing the divine nature as love." Put differently,

---

52. Personal correspondence.
53. Ward, *Priority of Mind*, 80.
54. Ward, *Religion and Creation*, 180.

if self-giving love is the highest form of Value, "then the creation of some universe may be *necessary* to God."⁵⁵

Ward has been wary here, however. He has not wanted to say that God is *obligated* to create any one world or, for that matter, the greatest possible number of worlds. The *necessity* he seeks to affirm is not constraint or obligation upon the nature of God *from without*, but rather free expression of this nature *from within*. Whatever constraints God finally has are *internal* to the divine nature as Love, and it is this nature that necessarily expresses itself through the being of the world.⁵⁶ In the final analysis, for Ward, God and the world *need* each other: "Without the world," Ward states, "God would not be all that God is. Without God, the world would not rightly be seen as what it truly is, the appearance of a spiritual dimension of being."⁵⁷ Moreover, without the "mutual immanence" of God *and* the world in this way, the supreme value of relationship and love would not be expressed at all. For Ward, such relational convictions carry both protological *and* eschatological significance. Here, his abiding confidence is again based in the supremacy of divine love and relationship. The same God that necessarily loves a world into creation, continues to love that same world into an eschatological culmination. As Ward has quoted Dante throughout the years, this is a "love which moves the sun and other stars."⁵⁸ It is this Love for Ward that ultimately guarantees "*the completion of the realized goodness of the cosmos.*"⁵⁹

---

55. Ward, *Religion and Creation*, 223–24 (emphasis added).

56. As Ward has queried through personal correspondence: "Does God necessarily produce a world?" He answers: "I admit that I am unsure about this, but I do finally think 'yes,' given that 'love' (sharing of goodness) is an essential feature of divine perfection."

57. Ward, *Religion in the Modern World*, 86.

58. Ward, *God: A Guide for the Perplexed*, 100.

59. Ward, *The Priority of Mind*, 55 (emphasis added).

BIBLIOGRAPHY

Cartwright, Nancy, and Keith Ward, eds. *Rethinking Order: After the Laws of Nature.* London: Bloomsbury, 2016.
Davis, Andrew M., and Philip Clayton, eds. *How I Found God in Everyone and Everywhere: An Anthology of Spiritual Memoirs.* Rhinebeck, NY: Monkfish, 2018.
Davis, Andrew M. *Mind, Value and Cosmos: On the Relational Nature of Ultimacy.* Lanham, MD: Lexington, 2020.
Nietzsche, Friedrich. *Beyond Good and Evil.* New York: Random House, 1989.
Ward, Keith. *The Big Questions in Science and Religion.* West Conshohocken, PA: Templeton Foundation, 2008.
———. *Christ and the Cosmos: A Reformulation of Trinitarian Doctrine.* Cambridge: Cambridge University Press, 2015.
———. *The Christian Idea of God: A Philosophical Foundation for Faith.* Cambridge: Cambridge University Press, 2017.
———. *The Evidence for God: The Case for the Existence of a Spiritual Dimension.* London: Darton, Longman and Todd, 2014.
———. *God, Chance, Necessity.* Oxford: Oneworld, 1996.
———. *God: A Guide for the Perplexed.* Oxford: Oneworld, 2002.
———. *Morality, Autonomy and God.* London: Oneworld, 2013.
———. *More Than Matter? What Humans Really Are.* Grand Rapids: Eerdmans, 2010.
———. "My Journey to the God of Personal Idealism." In *How I Found God in Everyone and Everywhere: An Anthology of Spiritual Memoirs,* edited by Andrew M. Davis and Philip Clayton, 63–78. Rhinebeck, NY: Monkfish, 2018.
———. *Pascal's Fire: Scientific Faith and Religious Understanding.* Oxford: Oneworld, 2006.
———. *The Priority of Mind.* Eugene, OR: Cascade, 2021.
———. *Rational Theology and the Creativity of God.* Oxford: Blackwell, 1982.
———. *Religion and Creation.* Oxford: Clarendon, 1996.
———. *Religion in the Modern World: Celebrating Pluralism and Diversity.* Cambridge: Cambridge University Press, 2019.
———. *Sharing in the Divine Nature: A Personalist Metaphysics.* Eugene, OR: Cascade, 2020.
———. *God and the Philosophers.* Minneapolis: Fortress, 2009.

Keith Ward's Response to Andrew M. Davis

ANDREW HAS WRITTEN A BEAUTIFUL account of my version of personal idealism, which I am very happy to accept. But as I read it, I am conscious that my view is very abstract, dealing with concepts of possibility, mind, and value, in rather abstruse terms, in a style that is far removed from the parables of Jesus. That is not surprising, for they belong to philosophy, and that is not an everyday topic of conversation these days (Plato thought you had to be drunk to take it seriously). But it does raise the question of what idealist philosophy has to do with Christian faith, and whether Christians need such philosophical concerns.

It is hard to know how much philosophy depends on Christian faith, and vice versa. There are few philosophers in the West who have not been influenced by the ancient Hebrew development of a morally concerned God. Jean-Paul Sartre's philosophy, for example, would not have existed except as a sharp reaction against a God whom he saw as always seeing and judging human lives. And there are few theologians who have not been influenced by the philosophies of Plato and Aristotle—the concept of a changeless and impassible God is more Aristotelian than biblical. Maybe philosophy and theology are more intertwined than some people think.

Jesus may not have been a philosopher, but he certainly believed in a God who created the world. That entails that the world of space and time depends on something beyond our spacetime, which freely caused the world to exist. So the physical world is not self-existent, but depends on a non-physical being beyond it. That is already a step towards idealism, implying that the mental is more real, and has more causal power, than the physical.

As early Christians reflected on the life of Jesus, they came to think that in some way the creative Mind of God had been expressed or manifested in the person of Jesus, which entails that the mental can be expressed in the material. In the Synoptic Gospels this is not worked out in a systematic way, but in the Gospel of John the idea appears that the *Logos*, the Word or Wisdom of God, had "become flesh," so that part of the world, at least, was identified with, or was a genuine expression of, God. Since St. Paul saw the church as "the body of the Lord," this identification of a supreme Mind with parts of the world was extended to include communities of humans. And some New Testament letters (Ephesians and Colossians) further state that the whole of creation (all things in heaven and earth) is to be united "in Christ." If this is true, then the whole universe is to be identified with God at some time and in some sense. This looks like a fully idealist view that the physical universe is intended to be an expression of the Mind of God, so that the history of the universe is the history of the gradual unfolding of the nature of God, which is essentially expressed in relation to created minds.

I am not implying that there is just one agreed or clear view about this in the New Testament. On the contrary, it is clear that there were arguments about it for many years, and what came to be thought of as the orthodox view was disputed by many. But the point is that there was not just one view from the very beginning, that the final view was only arrived at after many arguments, and that the Bible itself, or the recorded teaching of Jesus, did not settle the many questions that arose. The orthodox view was not the idealist view that can be seen in parts of the New Testament and that I support. Orthodoxy was more concerned to stress the sinfulness of the human world, and thus its utter otherness from God, which would indeed lead to its complete destruction and replacement by a new heaven and a new earth.

What sort of dispute was this? Was it theological or philosophical? It was a dispute about the content of divine revelation, so it was theological. But it was a dispute about human nature—totally depraved or partially morally disabled—and divine nature—expressed in time and nature or unchangeable and thus beyond time and nature. This was a philosophical dispute, which appeal to a source of revelation did not settle or even concern itself very much with.

My conclusion is that even abstract arguments about possibility, mind, and value are inescapable within theology as soon as we try to work out how Jesus is related to God, or how we can be related to Jesus today. Christian revelation, paradigmatically given in the life, death, and resurrection of Jesus, is not itself a philosophical theory. But to see it as a disclosure of the healing, suffering, finally triumphant love of God is to see it as a key to the nature and purpose of the universe. That requires a philosophical interpretation of the nature of existence, in fact a tapestry of many interpretations. Diversity and development, rational argument and disputation thereby become parts of revelation. To acknowledge this is to deconstruct the artificial opposition of revelation and reason, and perhaps to motivate a more tolerant and charitable view of the religions of our world.

DISCUSSION QUESTIONS

1. Evaluate Ward's claim that an ultimate Mind is the basis for all possibilities. What are some objections to this idea, and how might Ward address them?

2. How does Ward's personal idealism reconcile the relationship between Mind and Value?

3. In Ward's view, saying something is inherently valuable explains why it exists and stops further questions. Is this a valid foundational principle, or does it merely assume what it needs to prove?

4. According to Ward, in what sense do possible worlds exist? Why are some chosen to become real? Do you find his explanation convincing?

5. How does Ward reconcile the abstract concepts of possibility, mind, and value with the teachings of Jesus as presented in the New Testament?

7

Keith Ward on Comparative Theology and Religious Pluralism

A Catholic Appreciation

PETER C. PHAN

ISIDORE OF SEVILLE (C. 560–636) famously said that whoever boasts of having read all of Augustine, whose five million words have come down to us, is a liar. The same may be said, perhaps a bit less indisputably, of anyone who claims to have read all of Keith Ward. Such is his prolificity, which still threatens to continue for a long time, that one justifiably despairs of ever catching up with his latest publication.[1] Not only is Professor Ward's productivity superhuman but also the range of his academic expertise is astounding, covering almost all areas of philosophy, religion, and various religious traditions, theology, science, and ethics. Fortunately, his writing is not cloaked in Teutonic obscurity, despite his Kantian scholarship, but sparkles with wit and clarity. Perhaps it must be said, against academic indulgence in obscurantism as proof of intellectual originality, that a mark of the profundity of a philosopher's or theologian's thought is that his or her writings do not require a second reading to divine their meanings. One might not agree with everything Ward writes but one needs no hermeneutical jiu-jitsu to know what he means.

---

1. As of this writing, by my counting, Ward has authored fifty-one books of various sizes and levels of scholarship.

This essay deals with Ward's thoughts on comparative theology and religious pluralism. It begins with a discussion of Ward's early writings on comparative religion, from 1994 to 2000. Next, it considers Ward's recent treatment of religious pluralism. It ends with an appreciation of Ward's theology of religion and religious pluralism from the Roman Catholic perspective.

RELIGION, THEOLOGY, AND COMPARATIVE THEOLOGY

Ward is likely the first British theologian to have done extensive "comparative theology" before it became fashionable and influential in the U.S.[2] In a series of four volumes (1994–99), the titles of all of which begin with *Religion and*, followed by the specific themes treated, Ward investigates four main doctrines, namely, revelation, creation, human nature, and community, as confessed in primal religions and the scriptural traditions.[3]

Religion and Theology

In the first chapter of the first volume, *Religion and Revelation*, entitled "Towards a Comparative Theology," Ward expounds at length on the nature of Christian theology and comparative theology as a prelude to his project of a comparative study of primal religions and the scriptural religions of the world, mainly Judaism, Christianity, Islam, Hinduism, and Buddhism. Ward begins with a discussion of Thomas Aquinas's concept of theology (*sacra doctrina*) as universal and certain knowledge (*scientia*) which is based on the "articles of faith" deduced from God's knowledge itself given to humanity in divine self-revelation. While agreeing with Aquinas's statement that the purpose of divine revelation is humanity's "eternal beatitude," Ward rejects his overly intellectual and deductive approach to revelation and theology. Ward points out that not only there are many modes of Christian revelation besides doctrinal propositions but also diverse and multiple revelations (plural), a point that is central to his comparative theology project.

---

2. In the U.S., comparative theology was spearheaded chiefly by Francis X. Clooney and James L. Fredericks and developed by their students.

3. Ward, *Religion and Revelation*; *Religion and Creation*; *Religion and Human Nature*; and *Religion and Community*. For a study of Ward's thought, see Bartel, *Comparative Theology: Essays for Keith Ward*.

In light of the real possibility of divine revelation outside Christianity, Ward also takes exception to Karl Barth's, Emil Brunner's, and Heinrichs Kraemer's exclusivist restriction of divine revelation to Christianity and their condemnation of non-Christian religions and even Christianity as religion as a vain human attempt at self-redemption in opposition to God's purely gratuitous gift of salvation.

As to the possibility of arriving at certainty in religious matters, Ward holds that "one cannot argue for certainty in the sense of indubitable truth which any rational person must accept."[4] He believes that Aquinas was misled by Aristotelian rationalism to think that the certainty of faith is an objective matter of rational indubitability. Religion, Ward notes, is not a system of propositions to which faith is given, though of course there is intellectual adherence to a set of beliefs in any religion. Rather, he adopts Ludwig Wittgenstein's expression, "a form of life," to describe religion as a social system organized to satisfy practical interests and rooted in human needs, dispositions, and attitudes. Consequently, Ward proposes that there is in religion, instead of universally binding rational certainty, a "practical certainty" that reasonably compels a person to make an unhesitating commitment to a form of life and its practices. Ward points out that such commitment is what William James refers to as the option for belief that is "forced," "vivid," and "living." In religious terms, such an option and commitment is "conversion."

Another way to account for the uncertainty in religion is by appealing to what Ward terms "framework beliefs." These are "the scaffolding upon which a whole system of concepts is built, which articulates a practical way of life, and finds its primary use in forwarding that way."[5] It is important to note that these framework beliefs are neither certain nor uncertain and do not serve as irrefutable rational proofs of religious doctrines. Rather, like Kantian categories, they are inherent in our judgments and practices and provide the most general principles for interpreting human experience and resist unambiguous articulation. Generally, as Michael Polanyi argues, these framework beliefs remain tacit and are hard to make explicit. They are subject to continuous change as they are made up of different and shifting factors, such as personal emotions, moral inclinations, historical events, and cultural customs.

---

4. Ward, *Religion and Revelation*, 8.
5. Ward, *Religion and Revelation*, 10.

Thus, Ward does not subscribe to epistemological foundationalism, which maintains that it is possible to provide a set of basic self-evident propositions to justify belief. Rather, for him, what occurs in faith is an act of total commitment and trust to divine self-revelation perceived as the highest good:

> The fundamental premises are not theoretical, concerned with factual information and dispassionate. They are practical, axiological—being concerned with the search for and realization of fundamental values—and essentially involve commitment and trust. They are thus essentially tied to particular communities, with their own norms, practices, and focal objects of trust. One does not have an intellectual acceptance of universal and rationally compelling premises. One has communal commitments to disclosures of supreme value.[6]

Furthermore, the impossibility of providing an objectively indubitable proof for revelation also stems from what Ward calls the "ambiguity" of revelation. He notes that "God has not, in the working-out of Divine providence, seen fit to do so in an as clear and unequivocal way as could have been done."[7] God's self-revelation always took place in the languages of the people to whom God communicated, their thought forms, and their modes of expression, which are not always understandable to us and are subject to varying interpretations.

Revelation can be defined, Ward suggests, as "a Divine communication shaped to the interests and values of a particular society at a particular time. Its ultimate content is the existence and nature of a suprasensory good, a final goal of supreme worth. This content is expressed within a culture and history which facilitate a specific form of development."[8] Implicit in Ward's definition of revelation are two possibilities. First, not all framework beliefs are open to God's self-revelation; some may even be hostile to it. Second, not all revelations are perfectly received, or if received, correctly understood. It follows from these two features of revelation that "God will communicate different things to different people, and will in all probability be able to communicate more of the ultimate Divine purpose to some people than to others."[9]

---

6. Ward, *Religion and Revelation*, 29.
7. Ward, *Religion and Revelation*, 22.
8. Ward, *Religion and Revelation*, 24.
9. Ward, *Religion and Revelation*, 25.

In this understanding of revelation and religion, Ward argues that theology is more a matter of imaginative insight and articulation than linear deduction: "While propositional beliefs are essentially implied in religious practice, they usually have a provisional character, a diffuseness of content and an openness of texture, which allows and invites new possibilities of interpretation and of unpredictable interaction with other concepts. Theology cannot easily be regarded as the deduction of precise and definitive conclusions from a set of certain and literal propositions."[10] Since theology is based on disclosure rather than on communication of doctrines, its propositions are concerned to articulate and express such disclosure, "always provisionally and indirectly . . . rather than to define a set of truths which are directly and precisely descriptive of suprasensory reality."[11] It is important to note that such a view of theology applies not only to Christianity but also to all religions when they attempt to explicate the forms of life they commend.

Ward suggests that theology can fulfill its task of explicating the primal disclosure in the ever-expanding world-historical context in three ways. First, through the practice of dialectic or conversation, both synchronically with other viewpoints existing in the present time and diachronically with differing viewpoints in the past. Second, by discerning the pattern, model, or paradigm in which religions have developed. Third, by contextualizing the data of faith within the new knowledge in other academic disciplines such as the natural sciences, the social sciences, historical studies, and religious studies.[12]

In sum, given the probability that God has revealed Godself to different people at diverse times in several religions, that this divine self-revelation may not have been well received or correctly interpreted by a particular people, that it is impossible to provide indubitable proofs for the existence and meanings of such divine communication, and that theology is essentially a tentative, provisional, and exploratory probing of what may be termed "Mystery," there is a need for comparative theology to learn from the ways believers of religions other than one's own receive and understand divine self-disclosure throughout the centuries.

---

10. Ward, *Religion and Revelation*, 29.
11. Ward, *Religion and Revelation*, 29–30.
12. Ward, *Religion and Revelation*, 31–34.

Theology as Comparative Theology

In proposing doing theology *as* comparative theology Ward first of all addresses two objections against it. First, comparative theology is said by its opponents to be impossible since it requires competence in at least two religious traditions, while it would take the theologian a lifetime to understand even one thoroughly. In this endeavor, the systematic theologian runs the risk of being an amateur in religious studies. Despite this danger, Ward is convinced that it is high time to bridge the divide between religious studies and theology. For instance, he points out that it is impossible to understand who Jesus was unless one possesses a good knowledge of the Judaism of his time. This principle is also true of Christianity as a whole: "One cannot properly understand the mode of Divine revelation within Christianity unless one can set it in the context of human religious activity in general, for only in its widest context can one discern the true meaning of such revelation."[13]

The second objection is more challenging. Some theologians such as, in Ward's opinion, the Roman Catholic Aidan Nichols, and to a lesser extent, the Anglican John Macquarrie and the Orthodox Andrew Louth, maintain that Christian theology must be confessional, explicating the faith of a particular denomination, the truth of which the theologian has already accepted and lives by. Comparative theology, in their view, dilutes the Christian faith and weakens its certainty. In response, while acknowledging the validity of apologetics that attempts to argue for the validity of the faith of a particular community, Ward notes that there is "an intellectual discipline which enquiries into ideas of the ultimate value and goal of life, as they have been perceived and expressed in a variety of religious traditions."[14] This is comparative theology, which is differentiated from "religious studies" or "comparative religion" in as much as it is primarily concerned with the meaning, truth, and practical import of the religious beliefs of a particular religious tradition rather than with the historical, psychological, anthropological, or sociological elements of religious life and institutions.

According to Ward, comparative theology does not preclude commitment to a religious tradition nor reflecting theologically from a specific cultural and religious standpoint. But the commitment to a religious tradition can go hand in hand with criticism of it and its teaching authorities.

---

13. Ward, *Religion and Revelation*, 37.
14. Ward, *Religion and Revelation*, 40.

Theologians are not and should not be regarded as official spokespersons of their religious communities. Ward says that the office of theologians may often be that of a critic rather than that of an advocate. It is precisely in comparative theology that both the strengths and weaknesses of one's religious tradition can be perceived more readily and clearly.

Comparative theology, says Ward, shows that *"theology is a pluralistic discipline."*[15] In it, "people of differing beliefs can cooperate, discuss, argue, and converse."[16] Truth is best served by free intellectual inquiry and honest dialogue. Moreover, Ward believes that it is wrong to limit theology to one's own group and restrictive to define it by its denomination such as "Catholic theology," "Anglican theology," or even "Christian theology." Ward believes that it is preferable to say that "theology is the discipline of reflection upon ideas of the ultimate reality and goal of life, of God, and revelation. It can be undertaken by people of many diverse beliefs."[17] In this sense, comparative theology may be characterized as "revisionist theology," in so far as it stands ready to question the traditional teachings of religious authorities whenever an alternative seems preferable for a particular place and time.

In sum, Ward says: "Comparative theology must be *a self-critical discipline*, aware of the historical roots of its own beliefs; *a pluralistic discipline*, prepared to engage in conversation with a number of living traditions; and *an open-ended discipline*, being prepared to revise beliefs if and when it comes to seem necessary."[18]

Comparative Theology on Revelation, Creation, Human Nature, and Community

With these preliminaries on religion and comparative theology in place, Ward proceeds to examine how beliefs about revelation, creation, human nature, and community have been understood in Christianity and other scriptural religions. Needless to say, Ward writes from the perspective of a committed Christian and he wants to show how Christianity can be enriched and challenged by other religions. Space does not permit a full

---

15. Ward, *Religion and Revelation*, 45.
16. Ward, *Religion and Revelation*, 45.
17. Ward, *Religion and Revelation*, 46.
18. Ward, *Religion and Revelation*, 48. These reflections on comparative theology in *Religion and Revelation* will be complemented by Ward's summary reflections on "Christian Theology in a Comparative Context" in *Religion and Community*, 339–61.

survey of Ward's thought on these four themes; suffice it to highlight the most salient of them.

1. On revelation, Ward asserts that "there is an intelligible, natural, and defensible notion of revelation, the main elements of which can be found in a number of diverse traditions,"[19] which each tradition can and should preserve as its distinctive witness while engaging in an open interaction with others. In comparing the Christian concept of revelation with those of Judaism, Hinduism, Buddhism, and Islam, Ward stresses its similarities and especially its distinctiveness. The common element Ward discerns in the understanding of revelation in these religions is that it is conceived of not as communication of propositional truths about a transcendental being called God in theistic religions such as Hinduism, Judaism, Christianity, and Islam or about a state of complete liberation from ignorance and suffering in non-theistic religions such as Buddhism. Rather, revelation is seen as a self-disclosure of divinity or human enlightenment that commends a way of life leading to life's supreme good. Concerning what is unique and distinctive in Christianity, Ward stresses the radically historical character of Christian revelation which occurred fully in the incarnation of the Word and Son of God in Jesus of Nazareth: "God is manifesting the Divine Being decisively in this one historical life; so that this life becomes forever the image of God, as a historically purposing and redemptive power and value."[20] Christian theology of revelation is not based on a general philosophy of history à la Hegel but turns to "the history of the life of Jesus as the self-expression of the cosmic Creator."[21] It is also this emphasis on the historical nature of revelation that leads Ward to reject Cyril of Alexandria's "*anhypostatic*" Christology in favor of Leontius of Byzantium's "*enhypostatic*" Christology, according to which there is in Jesus, besides the divine "person" of the Word/Son of God, a human "person" or "subject," whose mind and will have been completely penetrated by the Word of God so that

---

19. Ward, *Religion and Revelation*, 1.
20. Ward, *Religion and Revelation*, 195.
21. Ward, *Religion and Revelation*, 208. With this unequivocal affirmation of the historicity of the divine revelation in Jesus of Nazareth Ward takes strong issue with Van A. Harvey's account of the relationship between history and faith in his *The Historian and the Believer*. For Ward's unusually extensive critique of Harvey, see *Religion and Revelation*, 247–58.

Jesus perfectly expresses what God is and perfectly expresses God as the supreme value.

2. In *Religion and Creation*, after a survey of what Judaism, the New Testament, the Qur'an, and the Upanishads (Judaism as seen through Abraham Heschel, the Qur'an through Mohammed Iqbal, and the Upanishads through Aurobindo Ghose) say about God as the Creator, Ward rearticulates the Christian concept of God in dialogue with the four traditions mentioned above. In addition, he reconsiders the concept of the Trinity in the context of recent scientific cosmologies.[22] Ward begins with a discussion of the three worldviews regarding God, namely, empiricism, materialism, and theism, and then argues that of the three worldviews theism is the most reasonable account of the existence of the universe. There is a metaphysical presupposition in religious, including Christian, commitment. This metaphysical presupposition is that "the whole physical universe depends upon and mediates a reality of supreme power and value, which can be apprehended in the empowering experience of salvation, liberation, or release."[23] Ward goes on to expound on divine power (creativity), wisdom, love, affectivity, and beatitude, five attributes affirmed of God in all the four scriptural traditions. Finally, Ward relates the Christian doctrine of creation to contemporary cosmological theories and explicates the Christian doctrine of the Trinity in relation to God's creative act, or to put it in technical terms, the relation between the immanent Trinity and the economic Trinity.

3. In *Religion and Human Nature*, Ward examines issues concerning human nature, especially the self, the embodied soul, rebirth, sin, salvation, and the destiny of the human person beyond death. Religious traditions under study include, in addition to Christianity, Hinduism (represented by the International Society for Krishna Consciousness and the Ramakrishna Mission), Buddhism (represented by Theravāda Buddhism and Tibetan Buddhism), Judaism, and Islam. Ward distinguishes four schools of thought regarding the self in these religious traditions: the self as purely spiritual (Hinduism); the self as one-self or non-dual (*Advaita* Hinduism); no individual self (Buddhism); and the embodied self (Judaism, Christianity, and Islam). Ward is deeply

---

22. For Ward's detailed account of the classical views of various religions on God, see his *Images of Eternity*.

23. Ward, *Religion and Creation*, 128.

aware that in matters regarding human nature and its ultimate destiny there is some agreement among the religions at the most general level, but at the less general level and especially at the particular level, differences among religions multiply and remain unbridgeable, even among the different "denominations" of the same religious tradition. Whereas in matters of fact disagreement can be in principle resolved by more attentive observation and analysis of the facts, in religion such procedure cannot be employed since religious matters do not lend themselves to observation and testing. Nevertheless, Ward is convinced that a resolute pursuit of truth is a moral duty "with a preparedness to understand as sympathetically as possible alternative views, and learn from them as far as possible."[24]

4. Lastly, in *Religion and Community*, Ward studies the various ways religions have organized themselves into communities and related to the societies in which they exist. In particular, he discusses Judaism and the Nation of Israel, Islam and the universal *umma*, Buddhism and the *sangha*, Hinduism and the *sampradaya*, and Christianity and the church. Ward proposes four "ideal types" of the relation between religion and culture/society: first, identification between religion and society; second, total separation between religion and society; third, interaction between religion and society in various modes, such as independence from, opposition to, validation of, and transformation of the culture and society; and fourth, religion as essentially a matter of choice for individuals and families without interaction with society.[25] According to Ward, Christianity as a spiritual community adopts mostly the third model in its relation to society, though it also follows the first model in organizing Christendom. As a church, however, Christianity carries out its mission as a teaching, charismatic, sacramental, and moral community.

In this fourth and last volume on comparative theology, Ward became increasingly aware of the issue of religious pluralism confronting Christianity. In placing the idea of a Christian community within a wider spectrum of ideas of the religious community, he notes that if there is a more underlying universal theme, "it is that religions in the modern world

---

24. Ward, *Religion and Human Nature*, 327.
25. Ward, *Religion and Community*, 1–3.

must unreservedly accept religious diversity, and learn positively to respect difference."[26] Again, in his summary of his elaboration of a Christian comparative theology in dialogue with other religions, Ward returns to the issue of religious pluralism and draws its implication for the church: "Thus the church must accept its role as being one religious community among others. It must accept plurality, though it will not cease to claim for itself a discernment of truths which are important for the salvation of humanity."[27] This frank acceptance of religious diversity and religious pluralism provides a natural segue to a consideration of Ward's later thinking on pluralism and diversity.

CELEBRATING PLURALISM AND DIVERSITY

The title of this section is taken from the subtitle of Ward's recent work *Religion in the Modern World*. Though religious pluralism has been the underlying motif of his early works, especially in his *Religion and Community*, Ward dealt with it as a theological issue explicitly only in his later writings.

Religious Diversity, Religious Pluralism, and Perennial Philosophy

There have, of course, always been many religions in the history of the world. According to Ward, this fact of religious *diversity* posed no theoretical problem as long as each religion's claim that it is the only true religion and that all others are false remains unchallenged. However, as David Hume has argued, religious diversity became a problem and gave rise to religious *pluralism* in modernity when there arose a strong conviction that none of the religious truth claims can be rationally substantiated and that therefore all religions are likely to be false. Of course, religious tribalism, in which one's identity is defined by membership in a particular ethnic or religious group, has not been erased in modernity, but now religious *pluralism* demands that a rational defense, and not just a tribal loyalty to one's religion, be given to religious truth claims.[28]

---

26. Ward, *Religion and Community*, 6.
27. Ward, *Religion and Community*, 358.
28. Ward, *Religion in the Modern World*, 9–11.

One way to blunt the force of religious diversity and pluralism is to assert that beneath all religions, despite all their differences in doctrine, experience, and behavior, lies a common core, a "perennial philosophy," an esoteric experience traceable back to some primordial tradition. This common core is said to consist of the experience of an ontological unity between the self and the ineffable divine Reality whose "divine spark" inheres in the human soul. Ward shows that such a view has been espoused with different nuances by perennialists such as the eighth-century Indian *Advaita* philosopher Adi Shankara, Aldous Huxley, Frithjof Schuon, and Huston Smith.

Ward believes that perennialists are right in saying that each religious community's grasp of the Absolute Truth and Supreme Value is relative to its level of understanding and limited by the finitude of the human mind. However, he believes that the mistake of perennialists is "to think that there is a way of escape from this form of relativity to a higher mode of absolute certainty, open only to a gnostic elite."[29] He contends that there is no "perennial philosophy," that is, some primordial and continuing, albeit hidden, religious experience and tradition. Rather, he says that "there is, underlying many religions, a rather general belief in the existence of a spiritual dimension, which is often thought to be of supreme value."[30] Of course, throughout history and in various places humans have cultivated a conscious relationship with this suprasensory reality by means of moral actions, mental techniques, and rituals, both public and private.

Four Religious Streams

Ward suggests that it is this general belief in and orientation toward the spiritual reality, and not some alleged primal common experience, that is the element lying at the core of all religions. He identifies four streams in which this general belief has been expressed: first, philosophical idealism, such as Vedanta Hinduism, according to which only the spiritual exists and the physical is its self-manifestation. Its goal is ontological union with the Absolute Spirit. Perennialists claim that this is the primordial form of ancient wisdom or perennial philosophy. Second, radical dualism between matter and spirit, according to which the goal of life is to be released from matter. However, contrary to idealism, this liberation is not for union

---

29. Ward, *Religion in the Modern World*, 64.
30. Ward, *Religion in the Modern World*, 65.

with the Absolute Spirit or Creator God. Instances of radical dualism are non-theistic Theravāda Buddhism and Jainism. Third, theism, according to which there is a personal Creator God with whom humans can enter into a relationship of faith, hope, and love and thus are saved. This stream is represented by the Abrahamic religions, namely, Judaism, Christianity, and Islam. Its concern is forgiveness of sin, reconciliation, and social justice. Fourth, philosophical monism, according to which there is only one reality, with the spiritual and physical dimensions co-existing. Its goal is to live life in accord with the inherent moral structure of the universe. It is represented by Chinese religions such as Daoism and Confucianism, which promote what Ward calls "the path of transcendental humanism."[31]

The "Critical Turn" and the Rise of Religious Pluralism

As mentioned above, religious pluralism, that is, the conviction that no religious truth claim can be proved by rational arguments, arose in modernity with its "critical turn." In addition to critical philosophy, which rejects all claims to absolute truth, Ward notes that the rise of the scientific method in Europe, the mechanistic worldview, and the evolutionary theory replaced the Aristotelian metaphysics with its fourfold causality, namely, formal, material, efficient, and final causes, as an explanatory model for natural phenomena. At the same time, the use of the historical-critical method in interpreting the Bible, which highlights its factual and even moral errors, questions its status as the exclusive authoritative norm for faith and opens up multiple new, non-Christian sources for religious understanding.[32]

Ward outlines the rise of religious pluralism in the works of Immanuel Kant, Friedrich Schleiermacher, G. W. Friedrich Engel, and Ernst Troeltsch, all of whom are skeptical of the existence of an ancient, perennial or esoteric tradition underlying all religions. For them, Christianity is part of a wider global history, and though they thought that (Protestant) Christianity represents the peak of religious evolution, they did not think that there is an eternal and unchanging truth in it or elsewhere. Rather, with the rise of historical consciousness, they thought that all cultures and religions are

---

31. On Ward's explication of these four religious streams, see Ward, *Religion in the Modern World*, 65–66. Ward points out that perennial philosophy is "only one tributary of one stream of religious thought and practice." Ward, *Religion in the Modern World*, 66.

32. See Ward, *Religion in the Modern World*, 67–69, 112–14. Ward cites the use of the historical-critical method by Rudolf Bultmann (70–79).

deeply involved in the continuously changing stream of interconnected causal influences. Religious diversity, and its correlative, religious pluralism, are embedded in all religious traditions.

The Pluralist Hypothesis

One outgrowth of the critical and historical turns is the pluralist thesis, of which the foremost exponent is no doubt John Hick. In his *An Interpretation of Religion*, Hick holds that religion is a human response to a transcendent reality (or realities) and that its various and different forms are shaped by the diverse historical and cultural contexts in which it takes place, giving rise to multiple religions and religious pluralism.

There is of course nothing exceptional in this description of religion. What Ward objects to is Hick's affirmation that the transcendent reality, which Hick calls "the Real," is, like Kant's noumenon, unknowable. Hick's assertion, Ward argues, leads to untenable conclusions. If the Real is Hick's description of God, and if it is totally unknowable, then one will not be able to discriminate between a religion that worships the true God and one that does not, nor can one determine whether the God two religions worship is the same God. Furthermore, if the purpose of religion is to lead people from "self-centeredness" to "Reality-centeredness," as Hick puts it, what would "Reality-centeredness" mean if one cannot be certain whether Reality is the supreme good or the supreme evil? Furthermore, doctrinal differences, even contradictions, are found not only among different religions but also within one and the same religion. Ward points out that there are over thirty thousand Christian denominations and doctrinal differences among them are not merely complementary but also contradictory and irreconcilable truth claims. Thus, even if one agrees with Hick's affirmation that religions are different ways of conceiving the Ultimate Reality, doctrinal differences, even those within one same religion, cannot be regarded simply as mutually complementary assertions about the ineffable Reality. If a doctrine is judged to be true, its contradictory assertion must be false.

Hick offers three possibilities for the epistemological status of religions. First, all religions are false (atheism or agnosticism). Second, only one religion is true (exclusivism). Third, all religions are more or less equally true (pluralism). Hick rejects the first two positions and favors the third.[33] Alan Race adds the fourth: only one religion has the full truth, but

---

33. See Hick, *An Interpretation of Religion*, 235.

other religions also have some truths, and these truths are "included" in the one true religion (inclusivism).[34]

Ward's own position differs from any of these four. First of all, truth, he notes, is the property of a proposition, and religions as such are neither true nor false: "They are mixtures of stories, rituals, institutions, ethical rules, experiences, and doctrinal truth claims."[35] Every religion, of course, has a set of truth claims. Each truth claim of this set of truth claims may be true or false, but its truth or falsity need not affect the overall adequacy of the entire set of truth claims. A particular religion as a set of truth claims can still be more or less adequate even if some particular truth claims of its set of truth claims are false or poorly expressed. As Ward puts it: "Not only is it difficult to pin down exactly what truth-claims many religious statements are making, it is also the case that, while individual truth-claims are exclusive, sets of truth-claims need not be exclusive of other sets of truth-claims."[36]

Thus, in Ward's account of religious pluralism, exclusivism is rejected since no one religion with its set of truth claims is said to be the only one true. Nor is inclusivism advocated because there is no claim that a particular religion with its sets of truth claims possesses the fullness of truth. Nor is pluralism defended since there is no claim that all religions are equally true and since one set of truth claims may have more truths than another.

Ward concludes his study of religious pluralism with a discussion of Wilfred Cantwell Smith, a historian and a specialist in Islam. He considers Smith's view "a quite radical form of pluralism."[37] First, Smith proposes that the term "religion" be dropped because it reifies into static institutions the changing, diverse, and complex historical processes of religious belief and practice at different points of history and in various cultures. He proposes to use "religious traditions" instead and highlights their cumulative character. Second, he rejects the concept of "perennial philosophy" with its affirmation of a past primordial experience and insists instead on the future dimension of religious traditions. Third, with the emphasis on the future of religious traditions, Smith holds out the possibility and desirability of a global religious tradition in which a different religion is not eliminated,

---

34. See Race, *Christians and Religious Pluralism*. See also Schmidt-Leukel, "Religious Pluralism in Thirteen Theses."

35. Ward, *Religion in the Modern World*, 145.

36. Ward, *Religion in the Modern World*, 148.

37. Ward, *Religion in the Modern World*, 157.

demonized, and excluded from the true faith, and a consistent effort is made to look for positive affinities among alternative traditions. Fourth, in this truly global tradition, it is possible to say that "salvation" is by "faith," reinterpreting salvation to mean a transformative and transcendent experience of a "surpassingly great Other" and faith to mean a passionate commitment to the best accessible and practical possibility, even if theoretical certainty is unavailable.

KEITH WARD: A CATHOLIC APPRECIATION

Ward devotes the fifth part of his book *Religion in the Modern World* to an exposition of five Roman Catholic theologians on religious pluralism.[38] In this concluding section, rather than examining how Ward appreciates Catholic theology of religious pluralism, I will do the reverse, offering an appreciation of Ward's theology of religious pluralism from the Catholic perspective. By "Catholic perspective" is meant here not only the official teachings of the Catholic Church, often referred to as the magisterium, with its varying degrees of teaching authority, but also the opinions of influential theologians, though their ideas may have been censored by the magisterium.

One of Ward's basic views on religious pluralism that Catholics would deeply appreciate is his understanding of religions not as sets of largely incompatible truths but as, to use Cantwell Smith's expression, cumulative religious traditions. The Catholic Church, despite its two-thousand-year developments and its expansion throughout the world amid vastly diverse cultures, should be eagerly receptive to Ward's view of religion. Ironically, however, it has tended to emphasize its nature as an institution endowed with one central authority (the papacy and the Vatican), a body of solemnly defined doctrinal propositions (the teachings of the papal and episcopal magisterium), a canonized complex of sacraments and rituals (the seven sacraments), and a list of moral precepts governing all aspects of human life. By contrast, by adopting Ward's concept of Christianity not as a block of unique, true, and superior beliefs and practices but as a community of believers among other communities of believers living out their commitment to the God preached by Jesus in diverse ways according to different cultures and circumstances the Catholic Church will be faithful to

---

38. Ward, *Religion in the Modern World*, 165–90. The five theologians are Karl Rahner, Hans Küng, Raimon Panikkar, Paul Knitter, and Peter Phan.

its nature as a *movement* of Jesus's disciples sent out to the whole world, powered by the Holy Spirit, to spread the good news of God's infinite forgiving and compassionate love as Jesus has announced and realized in his life and death, and in so doing, to respond to the ever-changing and new challenges of the time. It is what Pope Francis has been attempting to do with all kinds of church reform to focus all the church's activities on its central mission of announcing the good news and saving the earth from ecological extinction.[39]

Among the religious challenges of our time are no doubt the fact of religious plurality and religious pluralism. They undermine the Catholic Church's claim regarding Christ as the unique and universal Savior and the church as an exclusive community of salvation. It is well known that at the Second Vatican Council the Catholic Church underwent a drastic change in its understanding of its relation to other religions, especially as expressed in the council's Declaration on the Relation of the Church to Non-Christian Religions, known by its Latin name *Nostra Aetate*.[40] In brief, the Catholic Church abandoned its centuries-old exclusivist theology of religion and adopted an inclusivist one, according to which the Catholic Church is the only true church possessing the fullness of truth and the means of salvation, though non-Christian religions also possess some truths ("seeds of the Word") and means of salvation:

> The Catholic Church rejects nothing of what is true and holy in these religions. It has a high regard for the manner of life and conduct, the precepts and doctrines which, although differing in many ways from its own teaching, nevertheless often reflect a ray of that truth which enlightens all men and women. . . . Let Christians, while witnessing to their own faith and way of life, acknowledge, preserve and encourage the spiritual and moral truths found among non-Christians, together with their social life and culture.[41]

Though inclusivism marks an advance over exclusivism and is praiseworthy for its openness to and respect for non-Christian religions, critics have pointed out that the Catholic Church still evaluates other religions using

---

39. See Pope Francis's *The Joy of the Gospel* (*Evangelii Gaudium*) and *On Care for Our Common Home* (*Laudato Si'*).

40. For an English translation of this Declaration, see Second Vatican Council, *Vatican II Constitutions Decrees Declarations*, 569–74.

41. Second Vatican Council, *Nostra Aetate*, §2.

itself as the criterion of truth and value, and that ultimately inclusivism is only a milder version of exclusivism. Here, Ward's repudiation of exclusivism, inclusivism, and pluralism, as explained above, offers a more acceptable theology of religion. His point that the validity of a particular religion as a set of truth claims is not jeopardized by the fact that one or several truth claims of that set of truth claims are shown to be false is very helpful. The Catholic Church need not claim to possess the fullness of truth and all the means of salvation and superiority over other religions to preserve its status as a community of salvation. As such, it can and should learn from other religions to correct and improve its teachings and practices. Furthermore, it can and should recognize that other religions are authentic ways of salvation in their own right insofar as in them God has disclosed Godself as infinite compassion and love and shares God's life with their followers.

Finally, the Catholic Church and Catholic theologians have much to learn from Ward's practice of comparative theology. He has shown that the best way to understand Christian beliefs and practices is by situating them in the global history of religions and comparing them to those of other religions. Ward has taken care to point out that in doing comparative theology he is not doing apologetics for Christianity nor claims to stand outside or above religions and judge them from a superior Archimedian standpoint nor advocates some new global religion that could supersede all present religions.[42] Comparative theology has become a fertile subdiscipline among Roman Catholic theologians, especially in the United States, but there is still much to do, and Ward is a sure guide.

In summing up his life and work, Ward describes himself as standing within what has been called "liberal Christianity."[43] By that, he means that as an Anglican priest and theologian, he has a profound respect for the Bible and the church (Anglican) tradition but refuses to regard them as inerrant and immune to rational examination and criticism. In his view, in matters regarding God, the Bible as a record of God's self-disclosure and the church's understanding of it are "always partial, incomplete, and sometimes downright inadequate."[44] Ward's theology of revelation and religion is something Catholics can subscribe to.

It is proper to conclude this essay on Ward's comparative theology and his theology of religious pluralism with Ward's declaration of his faith:

42. Bartel, "Keith Ward: A Guide for the Perplexed," 195.
43. Bartel, "Keith Ward: A Guide for the Perplexed," 195.
44. Bartel, "Keith Ward: A Guide for the Perplexed," 196.

As I see it, the distinctiveness of Christian faith is that it sees its paradigm revelation as given in the life, death and resurrection of Jesus, seen as the historical and personal form of God on this planet. It sees God as a being of limitless and universal love, It sees human lives as trapped in bondage to desire, pride and hatred, but also as able to be liberated and united to God through the inner action of the Spirit of God. It sees the Church, the many communities of the disciples of Christ, as called to the vocation of proclaiming the good news of liberation and eternal life, and of serving the world in love. It sees the ultimate destiny of human life, and in some sense of the whole cosmos, as being taken up into the life of God, where all evil is redeemed and all good is conserved forever.[45]

BIBLIOGRAPHY

Bartel, Timothy W. "Keith Ward: A Guide for the Perplexed." In *Comparative Theology: Essays for Keith Ward*, edited by Timothy Bartel, 190–98. London: SPCK, 2003.

Harvey, Van A. *The Historian and the Believer*. Philadelphia: Westminster, 1966.

Hick, John. *An Interpretation of Religion*. London: Macmillan, 1989.

Race, Alan. *Christians and Religious Pluralism*. London: SCM, 1983.

Schmidt-Leukel, Perry. "Religious Pluralism in Thirteen Theses." *Modern Believing* 57.1 (2016). doi.org/10.3828/mb.2016.02.

Second Vatican Council. *Nostra Aetate*. In *Vatican II: Constitutions Decrees Declaration*, edited by Austin Flannery, 569–74. Northport, NY: Costello, 1996.

———. *Vatican II Constitutions Decrees Declarations*. Edited by Austin Flannery. Northport, NY: Costello, 2007.

Ward, Keith. *Images of Eternity*. Oxford: Oneworld, 1993.

———. *Religion and Community*. Oxford: Clarendon, 2000.

———. *Religion and Creation*. Oxford: Clarendon, 1996.

———. *Religion and Human Nature*. Oxford: Clarendon, 1998.

———. *Religion and Revelation*. Oxford: Clarendon, 1994.

———. *Religion in the Modern World: Celebrating Pluralism and Diversity*. Cambridge: Cambridge University Press, 2019.

45. Bartel, "Keith Ward: A Guide for the Perplexed," 198.

Keith Ward's Response to Peter C. Phan

I AM VERY GRATEFUL to Peter for his very positive exposition of my thinking about comparative theology and religious pluralism. I am particularly pleased that he is able to see my work from a Roman Catholic perspective, and find so much to agree with.

Peter identifies three points of possible agreement between a Catholic view and my own. One is that religion can helpfully be seen not so much as a list of dogmatic propositions as a cumulative tradition of spiritual practice, which is committed to proclaim a particular set of spiritual and moral values. Another is a recognition that many other religions are authentic ways of spiritual life, with much that may complement Christian insights. And a third is that no tradition or church needs to say that it alone has the full truth about God's revelation—after all, it is not surprising that, even though humans may know many truths about God, the full truth may well be beyond human capacities.

I certainly welcome this position, and it gives me the opportunity to say a little more about the place of the Christian spiritual tradition in the universe, which I believe calls for a fairly radical expansion—but not a total rejection—of some traditional Christian beliefs. The ecumenical movement is usually seen as concerned with relations between religions on this planet. But it is important to see that early Christianity was concerned not just with this planet, but with the whole universe.

Then it was considered that the earth was the center of the universe. The sun, moon, planets, and stars were set on spheres or circles around the earth, and heaven was above the sphere of the stars. But in heaven there were many different sorts of living beings—angels, archangels, cherubim, and all sorts of other beings that were superior to humans in many ways. Early Christians saw the incarnation of God in Jesus as a truly cosmic event.

Keith Ward's Response to Peter C. Phan

The New Testament letters to the Ephesians and Corinthians saw Christ as involved in the creation of heaven and earth, and so with the creation of many extra-terrestrial beings. And they saw the ultimate goal of creation as the unity of all things ("everything in heaven and earth") in Christ.

For Christians, then, the Savior of the world is not just a human person. The Christ, or Messiah, is not just a political liberator of Israel from her enemies, as some Jews thought. The novel Christian perception is that the Messiah is divine, a spiritual liberator of the whole universe from sin, hatred, pride, and greed. It was everything in heaven and earth—all human and extraterrestrial beings—who were to be liberated from everything that held them back from knowing and loving God, and being united in God. This was a radically new vision of the Messiah. The Messiah is no human being, but the divine Christ, the Word (we might say the "thought" or wisdom of the one God), who can unite created beings to God.

Of course, Christians believe that Jesus was the Christ, the Word of God "made flesh." Christ was authentically manifested on earth and acted through the man Jesus. But it is not just the man who saves. It is the divine Christ who saves in and through that man. Once we see that, we are free to say that the same Christ can save through many other beings on other worlds. In a world where there are no humans, perhaps no fathers and sons, there could be other forms of personal life, very unlike our own, and Christ might take such forms, which we cannot even imagine.

The divine Christ may take many finite forms, and in all of them his role would be to make God's nature and purpose known to every sort of finite being. So we can have the same belief as early Christians—Christ unites the whole universe to God—while we have a hugely expanded view of the universe. That enables us to wonder even more at the power and wisdom of a God who cares for millions of creatures in millions of galaxies and on millions of planets. This will probably be of little direct concern to us, since we will never get to other galaxies. But it will expand our conception of Christ, and enable us to see that his human form is not his only form, that humans are not the only inhabitants of heaven, and that what awaits us after death is inexhaustibly greater than we may have imagined. This is a view of a truly cosmic Christ, and it frees us from some of the anthropomorphic limitations that we may have placed on Jesus and on God, and encourage us to think that we as yet have much to learn of spiritual truth, and that there are many authentic spiritual traditions other than our own, though we may remain committed to the way of Jesus. That is the true ecumenical movement for our day.

DISCUSSION QUESTIONS

1. Discuss the strengths and limitations of Ward's critique of John Hick's pluralist hypothesis. How does Ward's view provide a more nuanced understanding of religious pluralism?
2. Analyze Ward's critique of Thomas Aquinas's intellectual approach to revelation. How does Ward's concept of practical certainty reshape our understanding of religious commitment?
3. Evaluate Ward's concept of "framework beliefs" and their role in religious epistemology. How does this concept compare to foundationalist approaches in theology?
4. How might Ward's notion of a cosmic Christ challenge one to expand moral consideration to animals, future persons, or other sentient beings?
5. Examine Ward's rejection of exclusivism in favor of a more pluralistic approach. What are the strengths and weaknesses of his argument?

Glossary

abyss of possibility. The vast, infinite realm of all potential states or realities that could possibly exist. It encompasses every conceivable possibility, both actual and hypothetical, and is seen as a necessary and intrinsic part of the ultimate reality. This is similar to the Platonic world of Forms.

Alfred North Whitehead. An English mathematician and philosopher known for developing process philosophy, which emphasizes the dynamic and evolving nature of reality.

annihilationism. The belief that those who are not saved by God will ultimately cease to exist rather than suffer eternal torment. It challenges traditional views of eternal damnation by proposing a merciful end to existence for the unsaved.

a priori. A term used to describe knowledge or justification that is independent of experience. It refers to knowledge that is gained through reasoning and logical deduction, rather than through empirical evidence or sensory experience.

axianoetic tradition. A stream of Western philosophical thought that integrates both Value (Greek: *axia*) and Mind (Greek: *noetikos*) as fundamental and ultimate principles in the nature of reality. It draws on the philosophical heritage of thinkers such as Plato and Augustine and aligns with philosophical idealism. Ward's personal idealism is a modern expression of the axianoetic tradition.

axiology. The branch of philosophy that studies values, including ethics and aesthetics. It explores questions about what is valuable, what is good, and the nature of value judgments.

classical theism. A form of theism that emphasizes God's transcendence, immutability, and impassibility. It portrays God as omnipotent, omniscient, omnibenevolent, and wholly other from the created universe.

critical realism. An epistemological position that sense-data provides knowledge of an objective reality, though this reality differs from how it appears to the senses. While Locke distinguished between objectively real primary qualities (e.g., mass, position) and mind-contributed secondary qualities (e.g., color, taste), modern physics replaces these with concepts like force-fields and wave-functions. Critical realists like Ward acknowledge an objective reality described by quantum theory's mathematics, though they consider this a veiled reality since we cannot be sure exactly what such concepts like wave-functions correspond to.

design argument. William Paley's argument that the complexity and functionality of natural phenomena indicate the presence of an intelligent designer, similar to how a watch implies a watchmaker. It is an argument for the existence of God based on perceived evidence of deliberate design in the universe.

divine temporality. The belief that God exists within time and experiences temporal succession. This view proposes that God is involved in the temporal flow of events and interacts with creation dynamically. It contrasts with the classical notion of divine timelessness.

empiricism. Empiricism in the British tradition in philosophy asserts that all knowledge originates from sensory experience. Relevant examples include John Locke, who argued that the mind is a blank slate shaped by experience; George Berkeley, who claimed material objects exist only as perceptions; and Keith Ward, whose experience of God in Christ led him toward a Christian view of the world.

enhypostasis. This term describes how a nature (such as human nature) is given concrete existence and particular identity within a person (hypostasis). In Christian theology, it is particularly employed to explain the union of divine and human natures in the person of Jesus Christ. According to this concept, Christ's human nature does not exist independently (anhypostasis) but finds its real and particular existence within the divine hypostasis of the Son, thus affirming both the full humanity and full divinity of Christ.

Glossary

exclusivism. The belief that only one particular religious tradition or belief system is true, and that all others are false or invalid. This view often entails the rejection of other faiths as means of salvation or enlightenment.

framework beliefs. These are the basic assumptions that support and shape a system of concepts and practices in religion. They guide practical living but are not provable or certain. Similar to Kantian categories, they are built into our judgments and provide general principles for understanding human experience, even if they are hard to clearly define.

idealism. Philosophical idealism is the theory that reality is fundamentally mental, immaterial, or spiritual. It posits that the nature of reality is closely tied to the mind and its perceptions, suggesting that the material world is either dependent on the mind for its existence or is an illusion created by the mind. Often compared with physicalism or dualism.

inclusivism. The belief that one's own religion is the true path to salvation or ultimate reality, but that other religions may also hold partial truths and can lead to salvation. This perspective allows for the possibility that different religious traditions can be valid and meaningful in their own ways.

interpretive hypothesis. A proposed explanation for a phenomenon used to make sense of observations or data. It is a tentative theory employed to interpret and understand complex information, guiding further inquiry and analysis.

Kantian categories. Kantian categories are fundamental concepts that our minds use to organize and understand sensory experiences. These innate, a priori structures, like causality and unity, are essential for making sense of the world and are not derived from experience but shape how we perceive and interpret it.

libertarian free will. The belief that individuals have genuine freedom to make choices if those choices are not predetermined by prior causes or divine intervention.

materialism. The philosophical view that all aspects of reality can be fully explained in terms of matter and physical processes. It posits that everything that exists is fundamentally material or physical in nature, and that all phenomena, including thoughts, emotions, and human experiences, result from interactions of matter. This perspective contrasts with idealism and dualism.

metaphysics. The branch of philosophy that investigates the fundamental nature of reality, including the relationship between mind and matter, substance and attribute, and potentiality and actuality. It seeks to answer deep questions about existence, identity, and the nature of objects and beings.

Mind. In Ward's philosophical theology, Mind or "cosmic Mind" or "divine Mind" refers to the ultimate, fundamental consciousness. It encompasses knowing, thinking, feeling, and intending. This cosmic Mind is the source and ground of all possibilities, realities, and values.

monism. The philosophical view that all of reality can be reduced to a single substance or principle. It opposes dualism and pluralism by asserting that everything is fundamentally one.

mutual immanence. The idea that the fundamental aspects of divine reality—Possibility, Value, Actuality, and Mind—are deeply interconnected and present within each other. This means that these elements are not separate or isolated but coexist and interact in a harmonious and relational union within the divine life. Each aspect is immanent (inherently present) within the others.

ontology. Ontology is the branch of philosophy that studies the nature of being, existence, and reality. It seeks to identify the basic categories and relationships of entities in the world, exploring questions about what exists, how entities can be grouped and related within a hierarchy, and the nature of their properties and relations.

open theism. A theological view that posits God's knowledge of the future as open and dynamic, rather than fixed and complete. It suggests that God knows all possibilities but does not have absolute foreknowledge of future free actions, allowing for genuine human freedom

open theology. A Wardian approach to theology that seeks a convergence of common core beliefs across traditions and learns from their complementary insights. It reinterprets beliefs based on new facts and morals, accepts diverse belief systems as long as they do not cause harm, encourages dialogue with dissenting views, and critically examines its own tradition. It remains sensitive to historical and cultural contexts, evolving with new cultural situations.

passibility. The idea that God can experience emotions and be affected by events in the world. This concept is significant in theological debates about whether God can suffer and be influenced by human actions and experiences.

perennial philosophy. The perspective, popularized by Aldous Huxley, that all major world religions share a common core of universal truths. It emphasizes the underlying unity of spiritual and philosophical teachings across different cultures and times.

personal God. A deity with personal attributes who is capable of relationships with individuals. This concept includes characteristics such as thoughts, feelings, intentions, and the ability to interact with creation in a personal and relational way.

personal idealism. The view that ultimate reality is a cosmic Mind (God) that is personal, conscious, and characterized by intrinsic value and goodness. Ward argues that the universe is a manifestation of this divine Mind, which is deeply involved in and relational with the created universe.

possible world. A way of speaking about a hypothetical or potential state of affairs that could exist. In Ward's work, possible worlds are not necessarily actual but exist as possibilities the divine Mind.

postulate. A fundamental assumption, principle, or presupposition accepted without proof and used as the basis for further reasoning or arguments. It serves as a foundational starting point for building theories and exploring philosophical or theological ideas.

practical certainty. The conviction that compels a person to commit fully to a religious way of life, even though it lacks indubitable proof.

process theology. Process theology sees God as dynamic and evolving, unlike traditional views of an unchanging, all-controlling deity. God influences the world through persuasion, allowing freedom and creativity. Similar to open theism, it emphasizes mutual influence between God and the universe but also suggests that God undergoes change and development.

Ramanuja. An influential Indian philosopher and theologian known for his interpretation of Vedanta Hinduism. He emphasized qualified non-dualism (Vishishtadvaita), which holds that the soul and God are distinct yet inseparably united, providing a framework for understanding divine and human relationships.

Glossary

reductio ad absurdum. A form of logical argument that seeks to disprove a statement by showing that it leads to an absurd or contradictory conclusion.

sentient. Possessing consciousness, awareness, and the ability to experience sensations, emotions, and subjective experiences.

standpoint epistemology. A theory that emphasizes the importance of an individual's social position in shaping their knowledge and perspectives. It argues that marginalized or oppressed groups can have unique and valuable insights into social realities due to their experiences.

teleology. The study of purpose, direction, or goals inherent in natural phenomena. It involves understanding the universe and life as having an ultimate purpose or design, often attributed to a divine creator.

Value. The intrinsic worth or goodness that is fundamental to the nature of reality. It is the quality that makes something inherently valuable or worthwhile.

Vedanta Hinduism. A major school of Indian philosophy focusing on the teachings of the Upanishads. It explores concepts like Brahman (ultimate reality) and Atman (individual soul), often emphasizing their unity or relationship, and provides a metaphysical framework for understanding reality.

Index

A Vision to Pursue 12–14
Absolute Spirit 108, 140–141
active learning 94, 102
afterlife 30, 35–36
An Enquiry Concerning Human Understanding 36
animal immortality 23
Annihilationism (glossary 1)
Anglican 2, 134–135, 146
anthropomorphism/anthropomorphic 32–33, 43–44, 65, 134, 149
Apostle Paul/St. Paul 127
Aquinas, Thomas 15–16, 32, 43, 46, 49, 115, 122, 130–131, 150
artificial intelligence 14, 16–17, 23
axiology 111, 119 (glossary 1)

Battle for the Soul 16
beauty 8, 25, 29–31, 45, 56, 64, 74, 98–99, 101, 104
Bible 89, 127, 141, 146
black existentialism 93
Brueggemann, Walter 45
Brunner, Emil 131
buddhism 136–8, 141
buddhist 5, 7

Calvin, John 47
capitalist 2, 100
Catholic Church 144–146
christology 3, 12–13, 136
community 3–6, 10, 18, 72, 90, 92, 100, 130, 134–135, 138–140, 144–145
community worldview 6

comparative theology vii, x, 6, 8, 91, 104, 108–109, 129–130, 133–135, 138, 146, 148
Concept of God 3–4, 37, 72, 137
consciousness 8, 16–18, 33, 64, 69–70, 74–75, 77. 86, 93–94, 96, 110–111, 117, 119, 137, 141
Conway-Morris, Simon 14
Craig, William Lane 54
creation 55–56, 60, 63–64, 68, 74, 77–88, 94, 96–97, 101, 123–125, 127, 130, 135, 137, 149 (glossary 2, 5)
creationism 7
creativity x, 5, 42, 57, 71, 88, 97, 100–104, 123, 137 (glossary 5)
creative ix–x, 6, 13, 24, 26, 28, 51, 53, 57, 64–65, 73–74, 78, 82, 86, 96–98, 100, 104, 121, 126, 137
Critique of Pure Reason 28
culturally relative 6, 22

design ix–x, 28, 36–37 (glossary 2, 6)
determinism 53, 92
Dialogues Concerning Natural Religion 28
Divine Action 8–9, 12–13, 78
divine attributes 48, 56–57
divine hope x, 44–45, 47–52, 54–60, 65
divine knowledge 80, 121
divine limitation 121
divine love 11
dualism 33, 140–141 (glossary 3–5)

ecological 114, 145
Emerson, Ralph Waldo 39

Index

Engel, G.W. Friedrich 141
Enhypostasis (glossary 2)
eros 98–99
eschatological 124
eschatology vii
exclusivism 142–143, 145–146, 150 (glossary 3)
Eucharist 10–12

feminist theology vii, 2
Fienberg, John 47
framework beliefs 131–132, 150 (glossary 3)
free will 17, 48 (glossary 3)
Fretheim, Terrance 45
future 9, 35–38, 42–48, 50–52, 54–58, 63, 69, 71–72, 74, 96, 100, 113–114, 143, 150 (glossary 4)

gender 5
God and the Philosophers 28–29, 110
goodness x, 23, 28–29, 31, 42, 45, 47, 50, 53, 57, 64, 73–74, 97, 101, 104, 110–111, 113, 119–124 (glossary 5)

Hart, David Bentley 80
heaven 3, 59, 75, 127, 148–149
Hebblethwaite, Brian 114, 14
Hegel 14, 108, 136
hell 121
Hick, John 142, 150
Holtzen, Curtis vii, x, 44, 63, 65
hope vii, x, 3, 23, 26, 34–35, 37–38, 42–60, 63–65, 75, 77, 104, 112, 141
human freedom x, 45, 48, 53–54, 123 (glossary 4)
Hume 21, 28, 30, 36
Huxley, Aldous 140 (glossary 5)

idealism vii, ix-x, 8, 22–27, 30–35, 38–39, 41–43, 68–69, 76–77, 80, 83, 85, 88, 104, 108, 112, 126, 128, 140 (glossary 1, 3, 5)
Images of Eternity 7, 137
inclusion 1, 7, 19, 94
inclusivism 143, 145–146 (glossary 3)

Incarnation 7, 11, 13–14, 49, 136, 148
intrinsic value 114, 119, 120–121 (glossary 5)
Iqbal, Mohammed 6, 137
Isidore of Seville 129
Islam 130, 136–138, 141, 143

James, William 131
Jesus 9–13, 21, 97, 126–128, 134, 136–137, 144–145, 147–150 (glossary 2)

Kant 28, 35–38, 43, 141
Kantian categories 131 (glossary 3)
Kraemer, Heinrichs 131

LGBT 1–2, 7, 19
Liberal 7–8, 18, 146
libertarian freedom 53, 59 (libertarian free will glossary3)
logic 5, 22–23
Locke, John 21 (glossary 2)
Louth, Andrew 134

Macquarrie, John 134
Martin, Adrianne 46
Marx, Karl 2
materialism 26, 38, 43, 68–70, 110, 137 (glossary 3)
medieval 29
metaphysic 8
metaphysical x, 1, 8, 24–27, 29–31, 34–35, 37–38, 42–43, 66–71, 78, 80–82, 87–88, 90, 94–95, 101, 104, 111–112, 115–116, 137 (glossary 6)
metaphysics x, 25, 29, 32, 66, 68–72, 75–78, 83, 87, 91, 94, 96, 112, 115, 141 (glossary 4)
methodology viii, 1, 10, 14, 19, 21–22, 26, 32
Mill, John Stuart 7
monism x, 76–77, 83, 85, 87, 141 (glossary 4)

Nichols, Aidan 134
Niebuhr, Richard 44, 65
Nietzsche, Friedrich 114

Index

non-attachment 7

Olson, Roger 48
omniscience 48, 54, 56, 65, 101
open theism vii, 59, 63 (glossary 4, 5)

Paley, William 28
panentheism 33, 89
passability 65
pedagogy 65, 88–89, 94–95, 97–99, 101–103, 107, 109
perennial philosophy 139–140, 143 (glossary 5)
perfection 27–31, 36–37, 42, 45, 56–57, 101, 124
personal God 33 (glossary 5)
personal idealism ix, 24–27, 30–34, 39, 41–43, 80, 85, 88, 104, 110, 112, 126, 128 (glossary 1, 5)
Plato 91, 98, 112–117, 119–120, 123, 126 (glossary 1)
pluralism x, 129–130, 139–146, 148, 150 (glossary 4)
Polanyi, Michael 131
Polkinghorne, John 94
Pope Francis 145
possible world 113, 121–122 (glossary 5)
prayer 4, 11
process theology 108 (glossary 5)

quantum mechanics 8, 23
queer theology / theologians 2

Ramanuja 33, 43, 85 (glossary 5)
Rational Theology and the Creativity of God 5
rationality 4–6, 23, 29–30, 34, 47
reason x, 6, 12, 22, 27–28, 30–31, 37–38, 40, 42, 44, 53, 64, 70, 86, 88–89, 91–92, 95, 99, 104, 111, 117, 119–121, 128
Religion and Revelation 4–7, 12–13, 130
religious diversity 7, 137, 140, 142
resurrection 10, 41, 127, 147
Romanus Cessario 46

salvation 2, 45, 59, 131, 137, 139, 144–146 (glossary 3)
Sandel, Michael 90–91
Schleiermacher, Friedrich 141
science vii, ix–x, 4, 8–10, 12, 18, 22, 64, 68, 94, 101, 111, 129
second coming 9
sentient being 7, 15–16, 23, 121, 150 (glossary 6)
sexuality 98
Shankara, Adi 33, 140
Smith, Wilfred Cantwell 99, 143
social justice 22–23, 94, 104, 109, 141
society 2, 22, 74–75, 94, 104, 107, 109, 32, 137–138
Socratic x
sovereignty 45, 97
Spirit 10–11, 77
  Spirit of God 147
  standardization movement 98–99
  standpoint epistemology 93 (glossary 6)
  suffering 16, 42, 45, 48, 50, 56, 73, 112, 122, 127, 136 (glossary 6)
systemic racism 8

teleology 37, 97 (glossary 6)
temporality 50–51, 54, 65 (glossary 2)
The Christian Idea of God 24, 30–32, 35, 37, 38
The Courage to Be 32
The Problem of God in Modern Thought 29
theism vii, 8–9, 15, 39, 47–48, 59, 63, 83, 137, 141, 142 (glossary 2, 4, 5)
Tillich, Paul 10, 32–33, 43
tradition ix, 4–7, 12–15, 18–19, 21–22, 25, 27, 29, 31, 33, 44, 66, 90, 100, 108–109, 110, 115, 117–119, 123, 129, 130, 134–136, 138, 140–144, 146, 149 (glossary 1, 2–3, 5)
transmission-based models 94, 102
transubstantiation 10–12
Trinity 6, 11, 15, 74, 137
Troeltsch, Ernst 141
truth claim 4–5, 139, 143, 146

unencumbered self 90–91

value x, 13, 23, 28–29, 31, 41–42, 64, 69–71, 75, 90, 93, 95–96, 100–101, 104, 110–114, 117–128, 132, 134, 136–137, 140, 146 (glossary 1, 4–6)

Vedanta Hinduism 140 (glossary 5–6)
Virgin Birth 12, 18

Whitehead, Alfred North 29, 42, 76, 96, 100–104, 120, 123 (glossary 1)
worship 4, 11, 27–28, 31, 142
Wittgenstein 4, 6, 25

www.ingramcontent.com/pod-product-compliance
Lightning Source LLC
Chambersburg PA
CBHW050820160426
43192CB00010B/1830